LAW FOR RETAILERS

The Legal Beagle keeps you straight with a guide to trading within the law

Bill Thomas

Cartoons by Peter King

2000

First published in 1996 by Management Books 2000 Ltd

This revised edition published in 2003 by Management Books 2000 Ltd
Forge House, Limes Road
Kemble, Cirencester
Gloucestershire, GL7 6AD, UK
Tel: 0044 (0) 1285 771441/2
Fax: 0044 (0) 1285 771055
E-mail: m.b.2000@virgin.net
Web: mb2000.com

Printed and bound in Great Britain by Biddles, Guildford

British Library Cataloguing in Publication Data is available

ISBN 1-85252-423-5

Printed and Bound by Digital Book Print Ltd

LAW FOR RETAILERS

bssa Guides for Retailers

This series of books is under the general editorship of Peter Fleming of PFA International - specialist consultants and corporate training advisers to major retail firms and organisations. The current list of titles is based on good practice in the Industry, and includes:

Managing Retail Sales
Law for Retailers
Retail Buying Techniques
Retail Selling
The Retailer and the Community

With suggestions for further titles in the series, please contact Peter Fleming on 01235 534124 or PFAInter@aol.com

bssa

The British Shops and Stores Association (**bssa**) plays an important part both in influencing and reflecting the views of the retail industry, with a brief to serve, protect and advance the interests of non-food retailers. In practical terms, that means lobbying both UK and European legislators, offering impartial advice on legal, financial and property matters and providing a helpline for day-to-day business problems.

The **bssa**'s training mission is to enable retailing firms to achieve productivity, profitability and excellence in customer service through their investment in people. Details of some of the short courses and seminars organised by the **bssa**'s Staff and Management Development department can be found in the Appendix.

The Association also provides a portfolio of business and professional services, which can save members considerable sums of money annually and, as a result, enhance the 'bottom line'. Services include a very competitive banking package and card processing service, the latter being a market leader in terms of rates offered; a Clearing House which allows members to pay their suppliers with a single cheque, thereby saving administrative time and costs; and an Insurance Brokerage, which specialises in the cover of shops and contents insurance.

bssa members, who are mostly small businesses, benefit from the economies of scale that membership provides, whilst at the same time receiving personal assistance in whatever area they seek guidance. With excess of 3,000 members, **bssa** is the lead association for the small business, non-food retailer.

Further information and details of membership are available from the Association at:
Middleton House, 2 Main Road, Middleton Cheney, Banbury, Oxon,OX17 2TN.
(telephone: 01295 712277, fax: 01295 711665, email: info@bssa.co.uk)
Look at our website for latest news: **www.british-shops.co.uk**

Contents

Preface

Of all the services which are offered by British Shops and Stores Association, providing help and guidance on retailing law is one of the most frequently used. Apart from the complications of the subject, customers are bombarded with information about their 'rights' from all sides – resulting in members contacting us for guidance about this most important area of business relationships.

This book covers most general legal circumstances likely to arise on a day-to-day basis and its clarity and style will ensure that it will have a place on every shopkeeper's bookshelf – and is essential reading for everyone in the Retail Trade. It is a unique guide, charting a practical course through the labyrinth of legal pitfalls and stumbling blocks with which every retailer is familiar. Read this book and you may save yourself a considerable amount of time, money – and worry.

John Dean
Chief Executive
British Shops and Stores Association

Introduction

I have written this book with one purpose – to make life easier for retailers. The law covers every aspect of your business and it is vital that you understand how it applies to what you do best – serving the public.

Although the amount of law covering retail distribution seems frightening, most retailers spend their professional lives without problems because they run their businesses in an ethical and common-sense way. The law-abiding have little to fear. I hope that those who strive to succeed but encounter problems should find answers here.

The law described covers England and Wales. Many aspects also apply in Scotland but I am not an expert in Scots law and traders fortunate enough to live north of the border should check with their own legal advisers.

I could not have completed the book without the help of Bob Thompson whose skill at disturbing carefully arranged piles of paper was second to none.

Bill Thomas

1

Organising Your Business –
The Legal Rules

Two different sets of legal rules

Retailing involves two different areas of law:

- First, civil law – which is primarily concerned with dealings between individuals (whether people or companies). Civil law covers the relationship by contract between manufacturer, wholesaler and retailer as well as between retailers and their customer. It also imposes liability in 'negligence' upon a trader if a customer is injured because there is something wrong with what was sold or the shop is unsafe or dangerous.

- Secondly, the criminal law – which, in general, is intended to control people who offend against society. In retailing it punishes traders who lie or cheat or do not meet reasonable standards.

Both areas are equally important, though what happens when one or other is broken is quite different. In a civil law dispute, a trader who loses usually has to pay money ('damages') to the winner as compensation for the broken contract or because he has been injured. When the criminal law is broken, the result will be that the trader is 'convicted', obtains a criminal record and will be punished – for example, 'fined' or, in extreme cases, sent to prison. The fine is paid to the State – because the criminal 'prosecution' will have been brought in the name of society.

Later, we shall look in detail at the way the two parallel legal arrangements work. First, however, we will investigate the structure of a business and the different ways in which you can run a retail shop.

In this chapter, we will look at and the way in which a retail shop operates. It is important at the outset to understand that the law applies to every aspect of any business where goods are sold or services supplied. People working in the business at all levels – from managing director to the newest sales assistant – will be affected. Because the law is constantly changing and developing, it is essential to keep up to date. Making mistakes or acting out of ignorance can have very serious consequences.

Methods of organisation

Sole trader

You may choose to run your business on your own. Whether or not you employ staff you are always the proprietor – 'the boss'. As a sole trader, you are personally liable for everything that happens. Contracts are made in your name; bank loans and overdrafts are your personal responsibility; any criminal prosecution would be brought against you. If the business fails, creditors are entitled to pursue you to your last penny; the assets of the business, your car, your house, your cat and dog and all your savings are all potentially at risk.

Many sole traders put valuable items – like a house – in their spouse's name in the hope that it will escape the clutches of creditors. It is perfectly legal to do this when the business is solvent, but there are great dangers if you do it when there are financial problems. The Insolvency Act 1986 gives the court power to re-open any transaction which it thinks you might have made so as to put valuable assets beyond the reach of someone who might make a claim against you as a trader, or with the intention of prejudicing such a person.

Examples of these potentially illegal transactions are:

- gifts or 'free' transfers of property
- gifts on marriage
- transfers at an undervalue.

Partnership

This can be a very effective way of combining skills. For example, you may be an ace salesman but your staid friend an excellent book-keeper. Individually neither of you has much to offer – but working together you may create a winning business.

Partnership is the name given to an 'unincorporated association of

individuals working together with a view to profit'. It may often be called a 'firm' or a 'company' although it carries unlimited liability. Prudent partners will take expert legal advice before starting out and consider having a 'partnership agreement'. This would specify, for example:

- how finance is to be provided
- the responsibilities and limitations of each partner
- how the business is to be run
- banking and credit arrangements
- how the profits are to be shared
- what happens if a partner retires or dies
- tax and pension schemes.

A small firm with up to 20 partners does not require any formal steps; the arrangement between the partners will be private. However, the Companies Act 1985 says that if there are more than 20 partners the firm will have to be registered as a limited company (see below).

There is a new statutory provision. The Limited Partnership Act 2000 allows up to 20 partners to set up in a form of corporate body, but with no shareholders or directors. Limited partnerships have to meet annual requirements for filing accounts and annual returns. You would need to take legal advice on the pros and cons.

There are special exemptions for law firms and accountants, and other professionals who are not allowed to limit their liability by incorporating; they may have hundreds of partners, but most retail partnerships have a handful only. Once more than half a dozen 'bosses' are involved as partners, it may be prudent to think about 'incorporation' as a limited company (see below).

Whatever the arrangements between partners may be, as far as the outside world is concerned each and every one has full liability for all aspects of the business. You may be completely unaware that your partner has signed a contract committing the firm to a heavy financial burden, but you are just as liable to the creditor as your chum. This is what the law calls 'joint and several' liability. To third parties, every partner is fully liable for the debts of the partnership.

Exactly the same rules apply about the extent of liability as to sole traders. The Insolvency Act 1986 would apply to partners who try to arrange their affairs to cheat creditors.

 WARNING: If you get into financial difficulty do not be tempted to transfer assets to avoid your creditors.

A limited company

This is a very common form of business structure. The key to the principal advantage is in the word 'limited'. It means that the liability of the members of the company – that is, the people who invest in it as shareholders – is limited to the amount of money they actually put in. So if you and your friends decide to operate as a limited company in which you will own shares, and you put up the initial money to acquire the shares and set up the company, your maximum financial liability will be limited to the nominal value of the shares. If the shares were actually bought and paid for, which is invariably the case for any going concern, you have no further liability to third parties.

Also, the limited company is a unique legal entity in its own right. It is important to understand that the limited company is quite distinct from its shareholders and directors. If Bill Thomas Limited is set up, that company will be separate from the man called Bill Thomas who may, coincidentally, own shares or be a director. If Bill Thomas Limited ceases to exist, because it has been 'wound up' or put into liquidation, there is nothing to prevent the incorporation of another company called Bill Thomas (1996) Limited – which may trade from the same premises and carry on the same sort of business, including the involvement of the same Bill Thomas.

However infuriating creditors and dissatisfied customers may find it, this is the law of the land. The very uniqueness of every single company is part of the attraction and is why so many small businesses are set up as limited companies. If the company has issued 10,000 shares of £1 each, and the five shareholders have paid £2,000, that is the extent of their liability.

In most small companies the main shareholders are the directors. New legal rules allow a company to have only one director although most small companies have several.

All companies must have a registered office, which is the address to which all official letters and notices will be sent. Many use their own premises or those of the company's accountants or solicitors. However,

some company directors choose an accommodation address (or a PO Box at an address) to which people rarely go. This can mean that urgent letters and notices warning of time-limits are not seen quickly and can result in expensive and even disastrous consequences.

 WARNING: Always select a registered office which is regularly attended by someone who is competent to recognise and deal with letters, etc.

 WARNING: Anyone who needs to should always be able to contact a director.

Any limited company incorporated in England and Wales has to be registered at Companies House in Cardiff. Scottish companies operate under a very similar legal regime but are registered in Edinburgh.

Information about limited companies and limited partnerships is available from Companies House, Crown Way, Cardiff CF14 3UZ and from the website: www.**companieshouse.gov.uk**

 WARNING: All directors of a limited company have special legal duties regarding the way in which the company is run and have to ensure that the company's accounts are audited and filed at Companies House. There are legal time limits for filing accounts with penalties (rising from £100 to £1,000) if you are late. Directors also face personal prosecution if accounts are late.

 WARNING: There is an important proviso. If, as directors or officers of the company, you sign guarantees in your own underlined(individual) capacity, you will still be liable if the company goes to the wall. This is because you agreed, as an individual, to stand by the debts of the company.

When you are thinking about the best structure for your new business, it is sensible to take advice from an accountant or a solicitor. You will need both as the business develops.

Raising finance is outside the scope of this book. All one can say is that, because of the risk of personal liability outlined above, you need to think extremely carefully before you sign any agreement relating to loans,

overdrafts, working capital, etc.

Business Names Act 1985

It is only right that the public should be able to know with whom they are doing business so that, if for some reason they want to take legal action against you, they may sue the right person. If you trade under your own name there is no problem; it is obvious who you are and where your premises are.

If you are a limited company trading from one place only, details of the registered office can be found from Companies House.

In any other case, if you carry on business under any name:

- in a partnership – which does not consist of the surnames of partners involved in the business (and the corporate names of any who are limited companies)
- as an individual – which does not consist of your surname
- as a company – which is not its full registered corporate name,

you must meet the very simple rules in section 4 of the Business Names Act 1985 and show the name of the sole trader, of each partner or the corporate name, and an address in Great Britain where documents may be served:

- on all the following:
 - business letters
 - written orders for goods or services
 - invoices and receipts
 - written demands for payment of debts
- displayed prominently at all premises to which the public have access so it can easily be read.

The second obligation is done in a simple notice reading as follows:

BUSINESS NAMES ACT 1985

Bill's Boutique

Owners: William Henry Thomas

Robert Thompson Catt

Address for service of documents

246 High Street, Diss, Norfolk, NR52 1AB

BUSINESS NAMES ACT 1985

The Pharmacy

Owner: J Robinson & Sons Limited

Address for service of documents:

37 Station Road, Penge, Surrey, SY43 8HN

 WARNING: It is a criminal offence – with a fine up to £1,000 – to fail to comply with these simple rules.

 WARNING: If you sue a trader who can prove that he was unable to make a legal claim against you because of this lack of information, or he suffered loss because of his ignorance of your true identity, your case may be thrown out.

Legal rules about running a business

In this country we are very informal about our commercial structures. Although a limited company has to be properly set up and registered, any sole trader or partnership can acquire premises and run a business from them. There are two main things to look out for - planning requirements and leases.

Planning

You can only use premises for a particular purpose if that has been authorised. For example, if premises are zoned for office use, you would have to obtain permission from the local authority to change it to a butcher's shop or a garage or a warehouse.

Leases

Many business premises are leasehold – that is, they are rented from the person who owns the freehold. All leases contain restrictions, the breach of which can give rise to heavy financial penalties. Never make assumptions that all will be well without checking details before you sign anything.

 WARNING: It is vitally important to ensure that the lease not only permits a business to be run from the premises but that the particular activity you have in mind is allowed in clear terms.

Business leases give security to tenants although the invariable 'quid pro quo' is a clause allowing the rent to be reviewed very frequently. Remember, too, that the first tenant under a lease remains liable throughout the lifetime of the lease, even though it is sold to someone else.

This legal rule was varied from 1 January 1996 by the Landlord and Tenant (Covenants) Act 1995. Tenants of business leases signed on or after that date will no longer be liable to the landlord once they have sold the lease to someone else.

 WARNING: The Act is not retrospective; tenants of all leases signed before 1996 will be potentially liable, despite no longer owning the property.

 WARNING: Business tenants must obtain expert advice from a solicitor specialising in this type of law.

 WARNING: Landlords have no legal obligation to allow you to give up ('surrender') a lease if the going gets tough. You may find that you have to go on paying rent for a shop that has closed and for a business that has no assets.

Opening hours

Whether there is any legal restraint on when your business can be open depends on what you do. Running a pub or selling liquor is hedged about with all sorts of rules – even though the old licensing hours have been greatly relaxed. Offices are under no legal controls; you can open for business for as long as you want.

In retailing, all the former rules in the Shops Act 1950 about so many hours per day, half-day closing and special conditions about employment were scrapped by the Deregulation and Contracting Out Act 1994.

Sunday opening

Until the middle of 1994, there were all sorts of controls on Sunday opening, many of which were openly flouted by large stores. There were silly anomalies, enforcement was uneven and it was said that the law was in disarray.

The Sunday Trading Act 1994 did away with practically all the regulations. Now all shops with a floor area of less than 280 square metres may open for as long as they want on Sundays. Large shops – with a floor area exceeding 280 square metres – may open for up to six hours between 10 am and 6 pm on any Sunday, so long as they give 14 days' notice to the local authority (which must keep a register of all notices).

There is only one restriction now: large shops are not allowed to open on Easter Sunday or on Christmas Day if it falls on a Sunday.

 WARNING: Your lease may contain limitations on your opening hours.

 WARNING: Even if there is no restriction, if you decide to extend opening hours, neighbours may claim that you are creating a legal 'nuisance' and may go to court for an 'injunction' either to stop you or to limit the time when you can be open.

Licensing

For certain types of trading you may need a licence – either for the premises or in connection with the product or activity. Here are some examples:

Activity	Apply to
Animal boarding	local authority
Cinemas	local authority
Dog breeding	local authority
Ear-piercing	local authority
Explosives	Health & Safety Executive
Firearms dealing	police
Intoxicating liquor	magistrates (and police)
Pet shops	local authority
Petroleum spirit	local authority
Poisons (non-medical)	local authority
Sex establishments	local authority
Tattooing	local authority
Theatres	local authority

Your shop and the public

There is no legal obligation to open your shop or to let the public enter. By allowing people to come in, you are granting what lawyers call a 'licence' and, although sensible traders will want to encourage customers, you are quite within your rights to lay down the terms of the licence. For example, you may:

- ban smoking
- refuse entry to dogs
- say that children must be with an adult
- insist that wheeled baskets are left outside
- ask customers to agree to bags (and/or clothing) being searched
- make people pay for anything they break.

Because the public's right to be in the shop depends on this legal licence, you may change the terms at any point and demand that someone leaves. If they refuse to go, you may use such force as is reasonable to make sure that the person goes although you cannot throw them bodily through the window!

 WARNING: Although you have wide discretion about whom you allow in – you must not discriminate against potential customers on grounds of sex, race or disability.

Safety

You have legal obligations to everyone who comes into your shop to make sure that the premises are reasonably safe and that any hazards are clearly indicated. (See Chapter 9 for more information.)

Music

Many shops have background music or a radio playing where the public can hear it. This amounts to a public performance and in order to comply with the law, traders must have the appropriate licence to ensure they are not in breach of copyright.

Composers and publishers are entitled to be paid when their music is

played in public. The Performing Right Society collects royalties and issues licences, the fees for which depend on the type of premises and the extent of music usage. Apply to:

The Performing Right Society Limited
Copyright House
29-33 Berners Street
London W1P 4AA
Tel: 0207 580 5544
Fax: 0173 331 2912
Registration phone: 0800 068 48 28
Website: **www.prs.co.uk**

In addition to the PRS licence, there are also copyrights in music which are quite separate. The people who made the recording are entitled to be paid. Their interests are looked after by Phonographic Performance Ltd to whom you should apply for a licence if you allow music to be heard (or videos seen). Apply to:

Phonographic Performance Limited
(or Video Performance Limited)
1 Upper James Street
London W1F 9DE
Tel: 0207 534 1000
Fax: 0207 534 1111
Website: **www.ppluk.com**

If you refuse to buy a licence these organisations can go to court and ask for an order banning you from playing any music.

 WARNING: Make sure you have the appropriate licence before you start playing music, etc.

If you want to have live music in your shop, you may need an entertainment licence from the local authority under the Local Government (Miscellaneous Provisions) Act 1982 as well as a PRS licence.

Summary of Key Learning Points

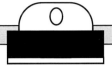

1. If you get into financial difficulty do not be tempted to transfer assets to avoid your creditors.

2. Always select a registered office which is regularly attended by someone who is competent to recognise and deal with letters, etc.

3. Anyone who needs to should <u>always</u> be able to contact a director.

4. All directors of a limited company have special legal duties regarding the way in which the company is run and have to ensure that the company's accounts are audited and filed at Companies House. There are legal time limits for filing accounts with penalties (rising from £100 to £1,000) if you are late. Directors also face personal prosecution if accounts are late.

5. If, as directors or officers of the company, you sign guarantees in your own individual capacity, you will still be liable if the company goes to the wall. This is because you agreed, as an individual, to stand by the debts of the company.

6. It is a criminal offence – with a fine up to £1,000 – to fail to comply with the simple rules about who runs your business.

7. If you sue a trader who can prove that he was unable to make a legal claim against you because of this lack of information, or he suffered loss because of his ignorance of your true identity, your case may be thrown out.

8. It is vitally important to ensure that the lease not only permits a business to be run from the premises but that the particular activity you have in mind is allowed in clear terms.

9. If you sign a new lease, you will be liable to the landlord long after you have sold the business and parted with the lease should the current tenant get into financial difficulty and stop paying the rent.

10. Landlords have no legal obligation to allow you to give up ('surrender') a lease if the going gets tough. You may find that you have to go on paying rent for a shop that has closed and for a business that has no assets.

11. Your lease may contain limitations on your opening hours.

Summary of Key Learning Points

12. *Even if there is no restriction, if you decide to extend opening hours neighbours may claim that you are creating a legal "nuisance" and may go to court for an "injunction" either to stop you or to limit the time when you can be open.*

13. *Although you have wide discretion about whom you allow in you must <u>not</u> discriminate against potential customers on grounds of sex or race.*

14. *Make sure you have the appropriate licence <u>before</u> you start playing music, etc.*

 Checklist

☞ How do we keep up to date with the law? Whose job is it to find out? Is everyone kept informed?

☞ Have we defined limits of authority for staff to commit the company – e.g. by signing contracts? Are there clear financial limits for individuals to spend? Have the relevant staff been told?

☞ How do we handle urgent and official correspondence? Is there a 24-hour contact system? Who has the responsibility?

☞ What reminder system do we have to ensure that Annual Returns and Annual Accounts are prepared *and filed* at Companies House on time?

☞ Do we display our name, address for service and other details on:
- business letters?
- written orders?
- invoices/receipts/demands for payment?
- prominently on all our premises?

☞ Do we have to get authority or a licence from the local authority? Is it up to date?

☞ Do our trading hours meet the legal requirements?

☞ Do we play music on the premises? Have we obtained the necessary licence? Is it still in force?

2

Making A Contract – The Preliminaries

Before we look closely at the way contracts are made there are several points to clear out of the way.

Displaying goods

The public usually believe that they have a right to buy anything that is on display in a retailer's shop. They do not. You are not obliged to sell anything. Having merchandise arranged around the premises for potential customers to look at is legally an 'invitation to treat' – literally an invitation to buyers to come in and make an offer. A customer cannot insist on buying any particular item or 'the one in the window'.

 WARNING: There is an overlap with criminal law here; you can refuse to sell something, but if it is wrongly described or priced, you may be guilty of an offence – even though no one lost money or was prejudiced (see Chapter 7).

Advertising

Although there are some laws covering advertising – especially for credit (see Chapter 6) – there is no specific Act saying what may or may not be in an advertisement. In the UK the whole field is controlled by voluntary action, mainly by the Advertising Standards Authority whose abiding principle is that:

- All advertisements should be legal, decent, honest and truthful.

In 1995 there was a new edition of the British Codes of Advertising and Sales Promotion which contain the rules which the advertising industry has agreed for things like:

- advertisements in newspapers, magazines, leaflets etc
- cinema and video commercials
- sales promotions
- advertisement promotions.

Television and radio commercials are covered by:

- Independent Television Commission Code of Advertising Standards and Practice
- Radio Authority Code of Advertising Standards and Practice.

Mail order is covered by several Codes:

- Mail Order Traders' Association Code of Practice
- Direct Mail Producers' Association Code of Practice
- Direct Marketing Association Code of Practice.

Oddly, although there are criminal sanctions (under the Trade Descriptions Act 1968 and the Consumer Credit Act 1974) for statements in adverts that are plainly untrue, the only set of regulations which are enforced by the State (as opposed to voluntary control through the sort of codes described above) are the:

- Control of Misleading Advertisements Regulations 1988 (which implement a Directive from the European Union).

These require the Director General of Fair Trading (for press adverts) and the Independent Television Commission and the Radio Authority (for commercials on TV and radio) to consider complaints about press adverts which are 'misleading'. The sanction is to ask the court to grant an 'injunction' banning the advert. These powers have only been used a handful of times.

Making a contract

Many aspects of retail trading are set out in the Sale of Goods Act 1979, which contains a straightforward code in a logical sequence. Later we will look in detail at the most important parts of this Act. However, the rules

about making contracts are not to be found in any Act of Parliament but have simply been developed over the centuries as part of the common law.

There are three essential ingredients for a valid contract:

- an offer
- an unconditional acceptance
- 'consideration'.

'Consideration' can be made very complicated by lawyers. For our purposes it is simplest to accept that, in the case of contracts between retailer and suppliers or retailers and their customers, it means the price, because each side in this sort of commercial deal intends to create a legal relationship and knows that money will change hands – otherwise the parties would not be negotiating.

The principles of 'offer' and 'acceptance' apply to every contract – from the sale of a box of matches to the supply of a cruise liner. Reading the law reports, it is remarkable how often the basic situation is ignored or misunderstood.

- 'Will you sell me this table for £200 including delivery?' is a typical offer from a customer.
- The trader may either say:
 'Yes' – at which moment a valid, binding contract comes into existence
 'No' (refusing, for example, to sell the item in the window that the customer is insisting on buying) – in which case there is no contract.

There is a third situation: the trader may introduce conditions.

- 'Yes, I will sell the table, but only if you transport it yourself'.

In legal jargon, by this statement the trader 'refuses' the customer's original offer to buy, but makes a 'counter-offer' to sell, so throwing the ball back to the customer.

He then has three choices:

- to 'accept' the counter-offer, whereupon a contract comes into existence
- to refuse = no contract
- to make another 'counter-offer' – 'I will buy it if you can assure me that it will go on looking like wood'.

You will understand by now that this third option returns the initiative to the trader who may say:

- 'Yes' = contract
- 'No' = no contract
- 'Yes – but...' = negotiations still open for further counter-offers, etc.

When it is all written down it looks rather complicated but as there is a world of difference between there being a contract or there not being one, it is very important to be able to analyse what happened during the discussions.

Retailers have to treat their customers fairly; the law says that they cannot escape their liability. However, their rights against suppliers may be restricted. If things go wrong, the consequences can be catastrophic. This makes it all the more vital to know whether or not a contract exists.

Contracts between suppliers and retailers

The negotiations between retailers and the manufacturers, wholesalers and other suppliers may be even more complicated. We shall therefore spend some time seeing how a commercial contract comes into existence.

It is absolutely vital that a company sets up a method of making contracts which all relevant staff know and understand and are instructed to follow without any variation. This is easier said than done, and orders come in by phone, fax and/or telex; all sorts of people – sometimes merely because they were passing a ringing phone – do things which irrevocably commit a company to a contract. It may be worth losing an order rather than finding that you are stuck with a bad debt.

It is most unusual for buyers of goods to impose their terms of purchase on their suppliers. They may think that they have done so (as we will see below) but unless they are large enterprises with skilled legal and negotiating departments, the usual rule in retailing is that the supplier's terms prevail.

 WARNING: In commercial contracts 'terms and conditions' play a large role. Whose terms apply depends on the way the contract was made.

'Offers' to buy are more usual than 'offers' to sell – that is the way of the world. In retail distribution, therefore, the offer usually comes from the

retailer who places an order with a supplier.

There are several common situations.

First, a retailer (P) sends an order to buy goods from a supplier (S). P's order has his terms and conditions of purchase (TCP) printed on the back. On receipt of the order, S sends the goods. Some time after delivery S sends an invoice with his terms and conditions of sale (TCS) on the back. The legal analysis is:

- P's order = 'offer' to buy on his terms TCP
- delivery by S = 'acceptance' of the order and its terms TCP = binding contract
- purchaser's terms TCP govern the contract.

Secondly, a retailer (P) sends an order to buy goods from a supplier (S). P's order has his terms and conditions of purchase (TCP) printed on the back. On receipt of the order, S sends an acknowledgement of order containing his terms and conditions of sale (TCS). Pausing for a moment, let us look at the legal situation:

- P's order = 'offer' to buy on his terms TCP
- S's acknowledgement = 'refusal' and 'counter-offer' to sell on TCS.

What happens next?

- P does nothing = refusal = no contract
- P does nothing; S delivers goods; P refuses to accept = no contract
- P does nothing; S delivers goods; P takes delivery and pays = acceptance = contract; supplier's terms TCS govern the contract
- P formally accepts S's TCS = contract; supplier's terms TCS govern the contract.

Thirdly, a retailer P sends an order to buy goods containing his terms and conditions of purchase (TCP). The supplier S makes the goods and sends them off with a delivery note or invoice containing his terms and conditions of sale (TCS). P takes delivery and pays the invoice. Here is the legal analysis:

- P's order = 'offer' to buy on his TCP
- S never formally 'accepts' the offer, but delivers the goods with the TCS = 'counter offer' to sell

- P 'accepts' the counter offer by taking delivery; supplier's terms TCS govern the contract.

Fourthly, P sends a multi-part order containing his TCP with a tear-off 'acknowledgement' or 'acceptance' page. S helpfully detaches this, signs, dates and returns it to P.

- P's order = 'offer' to buy on his TCP
- S's signature of acknowledgement page = 'acceptance' on P's terms TCP = contract; no matter what later documents S may send purchaser's terms TCP govern the contract.

 WARNING: *The law says that to be effective, terms and conditions must be imposed or incorporated into the contract by being drawn to the buyer's attention at or before the time it is made. If they are not, they have no legal effect.*

It is because of this that business people try so hard to make sure that, whether buyer or seller, their terms apply. What sometimes looks like a snowstorm of paper has been called the 'battle of the forms' as each strives to be in charge.

Another familiar situation is this. P may phone or fax an order and refer to 'the usual terms' by which he means his TCP, but the supplier thinks refers to his TCS. Here there is a serious legal problem. It is also a symptom of the times that people using fax machines (and copiers) almost always fail to copy any material printed on the back of a sheet of paper, which often means that contract terms which might have been vital are never incorporated into a contract.

Course of trading

Once a supplier and a retailer have been dealing with each other regularly, it is said that a 'course of dealing' has developed. In the event of a legal dispute, the court will assume that the method of trading which came into existence when the very first contract was made will apply in all subsequent cases. That is why it is so important to get things right at the start.

To deal with this point when approached by a new retail customer many suppliers will send two copies of a letter setting out the terms and conditions of supply. They require the retailer's managing director or

proprietor to sign one copy and return it confirming that he understands that those are the terms (TCS) which will govern all contracts.

If, when the first order arrives, it is accompanied by the retailer's TCP (they always are) the supplier should immediately send an acknowledgement containing the TCS and referring to the letter signed by the retailer. He should be asked to confirm – before the order is processed – that he understands that he is solely dealing on the TCS.

WARNING: Do not sign any document unless you understand the legal consequences of doing so.

As far as the outside world is concerned, it does not matter that you have clear internal instructions about who may or may not sign papers. Any member of your staff may, by signing an invoice, delivery note or acknowledgement form, bind you and your company. It is therefore vital that all employees are trained – and constantly reminded – that only designated people can sign any document. After all, you do not allow all and sundry to sign cheques.

It may all seem a rigmarole and new customers may think that it reflects on their integrity; your staff may think that it is just a lot of legal mumbo-jumbo. Do not be dissuaded. It is far better to lose one difficult customer than to have a lengthy and expensive legal battle about whose terms were paramount.

WARNING: Make sure that employees know who is empowered to make contracts.

Contracts between retailers and their customers

Because of the transitory nature of shopping, most contracts between retailers and the public are not in writing but are by conduct or word of mouth. The same ingredients of 'offer' and 'acceptance' apply, of course, and generally the offer comes from the customer because he wants to buy something.

Where the goods are already available and can be taken away there and then, the customer may say: 'I would like this handbag'; 'a pound of rump steak'; 'a dozen eggs'. The trader will either say 'yes' – at which moment a binding contract comes into existence; 'no' – then there is no contract;

or he may impose conditions by saying that the eggs are not free-range, or that he has no rump steak but some topside.

Here the same rules about 'counter-offers' apply; the ball is tossed back to the customer who may choose whether to go on discussing the transaction or abandon it and go home.

Supermarkets and self-service

Having goods on a shelf for customers to look at is not an 'offer' in a normal shop; it is what is called an 'invitation to treat'. In a supermarket or self-service store, taking goods from a display and putting them in a trolley or basket is not an 'offer' by the customer because he can always change his mind and put them back. The goods are therefore still the property of the shop or store and if broken are its responsibility, not that of the customer – unless he flung them at the wall of course.

The 'offer' is made when the customer arrives at the checkout (see below). Many people think that there has to be payment for there to be a contract. This is not the case. The law takes it as read that money is involved. The customer knows that he will have to pay for what he is buying and the retailer would not be selling things if he was not going to be paid for them.

There may well be discussion about both the amount to be paid and the mechanics of payment – cash, cheque, credit, etc. – but the contract is made when the negotiation comes to an end and an offer is matched by an unconditional acceptance.

This has important legal consequences because, where this type of contract is made, the instant when the contract comes into being is the same moment when the ownership of the goods changes hands. From that moment on, the customer – not the retailer – is the owner of the goods. If a customer offers to buy a table, and his offer is accepted, it now becomes his table. Should someone else have sold the same table half-an-hour before, you have a problem.

 WARNING: Make certain that staff – particularly those on commission and part-timers – do not sell any goods unless they know what they are doing.

Goods which have to be ordered

There are many types of products in a shop which may be merely on display; the trader will not sell them but will take orders for similar goods.

In these situations, putting things in writing is much more common. A customer may want to buy furniture. He sees a suite which takes his fancy but wants it in a different fabric.

The salesperson will write down the details and will discuss delivery. Has a contract been made? Yes, in the same way as if the goods were ready to take away. The customer indicated that he wanted to buy something similar to what was in the shop; the trader said that it was available, if ordered, and the customer agreed to place an order.

The legal analysis is:

- customer's questions almost certainly *not* offer
- retailer's statement that goods could be ordered = 'offer' to sell on the agreed terms as to style, fabric, delivery, price, etc.
- customer's agreement = 'acceptance'
- contract made for sale of 'future goods'.

The term 'future goods' is important because of the transfer of ownership. We have seen that for goods ready for immediate sale (what the Sale of Goods Act 1979 calls 'specific goods') ownership changes hands at the moment the contract is made. But where goods do not even exist – because they will not until the manufacturer has received the order and made the suite to match the customer's requirements – it is obviously not possible for ownership to be discussed, let alone transferred.

Transfer of ownership

Section 18 of the Sale of Goods Act 1979 contains a series of formulae for deciding when property (which is what lawyers call 'ownership') is to be transferred when there is no prior agreement between the parties to a contract.

Rule 1 deals with the everyday situation described above where a shopper buys something in a shop, pays for it and takes it away.

- Where there is an unconditional contract for the sale of specific goods in a deliverable state the property passes to the buyer when the contract is made, and it is immaterial whether the time of payment or the time of delivery or both is postponed.

Rule 2 also deals with 'specific goods' and says that where the seller has to do something to put them in a 'deliverable state' – which means, perhaps, assemble them, or do a pre-delivery inspection – property does not pass until the something has been done and the buyer has notice that it has been done.

For 'future goods' it is logical that the time for transfer of ownership is deferred until the goods are ready and Rule 5 recognises this:

- Where there is a contract for the sale of unascertained or future goods by description, and goods of that description and in a deliverable state are unconditionally appropriated to the contract (either by the seller with the assent of the buyer or by the buyer with the assent of the seller), the property then passes to the buyer.

Rule 5 goes on to say that the assent (e.g. agreement) can be express or implied, and may be given before or after 'appropriation', which means that the buyer or seller actually discuss the time when the goods are assumed to be ready and correspond with the contract, or that what happens is assumed to be what they wanted.

As 'appropriation' may take place at unexpected times and places – for example, when the manufacturer puts the goods on a lorry for delivery to the retailer (or, indeed, to the customer's home) – the consequences can be unsatisfactory.

Legal relationship between customer, retailer and supplier

When you make a contract with your customer for 'future goods', the onus is on you to be able to produce what the customer ordered. He may pay you some money – all or part of the price. You then place an order with your supplier. That is a second contract for the same goods, this time between you and the manufacturer. The supplier has the same legal duty to you – to come up with the goods in exchange for some money.

What happens if the manufacturer is unable to supply the goods, or if he goes out of business? As between you and the manufacturer there is a breach of contract, you are entitled to 'damages' if he simply fails to produce what you ordered. If he has gone into liquidation it is most unlikely that you will ever get the goods; any money that you have paid will be swallowed by the liquidator.

On the other hand, you are still in business and have legal duties to your customer. Your inability to supply the goods is also a breach of your contract with him. You may be able to show that because the manufacturer went bust the contract was 'frustrated'. In any event, if you have received money from the customer you must refund it – even if you have paid it along the chain to the fellow who is in liquidation.

Risk

The usual rule under the Sale of Goods Act 1979 is that risk passes when ownership changes hands – unless the parties have agreed otherwise. This will apply when you order goods from your suppliers. In the example of the furniture order, this legal rule means that the customer may well have become the owner quite unwittingly, and if the lorry crashes on the journey, it is the customer who has to stand the loss.

If the delivery is delayed through the fault of either seller or buyer, the goods are at the risk of the party at fault at least for any loss resulting from the delay. Where the goods are to be delivered by the seller anywhere other than his own premises, the buyer takes the risk of any deterioration likely to occur during transit.

However, the law has changed for consumer sales. The Sale and Supply of Goods to Consumers Regulations 2002 (see below page 93) amended section 20 of the Sale of Goods Act 1979. Now, goods in a consumer sale remain at the risk of the seller until they are delivered to the consumer.

 WARNING: Make sure that you understand when you take on responsibility for risk.

Contracts by conduct

There are millions of contracts made every day where not a word is exchanged between customer and trader. Buying a newspaper by taking one from the pile and handing over the right money is one example. Supermarket shopping is another. There one fills up a trolley and, on reaching the checkout, the goods are rung up or passed across a scanner. The first words spoken may be the total which one has to pay.

The legal analysis is:

- goods stacked on shelves = 'invitation to treat' (see Chapter 1)
- customer selects goods = no legal significance
- proffering goods at checkout = 'offer' by customer
- ringing up/scanning = 'acceptance' by trader = unconditional contract.

There is probably a separate contract for each item of goods because the customer can change his mind at any stage and abandon the half-empty trolley without any legal problems.

Contracts with machines

For many years it was thought that one 'offered' to make a contract by inserting money in a machine and that 'acceptance' took place when the machine issued a ticket or spat out the chocolate bar or lifted a barrier to enable one to pass through.

In 1971 the Court of Appeal gave a judgment on this question for the first time and held that the 'offer' was made by the owner of the machine making it available to perform its function. The customer 'accepts' by putting money in it. The contract comes into existence at that instant.

(Thornton v. Shoe Lane Parking Ltd (1971)).

The point in time when a contract is born is of vital importance when there is any argument about the legal effect of any terms and conditions which the owner of the machine hopes to impose on the public. As you will have seen, these only apply if they have been 'incorporated' at or before the time the contract is made.

Despite legal advice, the operators of many types of machine – in carparks, railway stations and cloakrooms, for example – do not display their small print anywhere near the ticket machine. Often it is only possible to see it after the ticket has been bought; in this case the terms have no legal effect at all. Or the ticket may be printed with something like 'issued subject to the company's terms and conditions'. Here, only if the full terms are clearly visible before the money is inserted will they have any validity.

Distance Selling

There are special rules for retailers who sell goods to consumers by 'distance communication'. This means selling by telephone, mail order, fax, digital television, or over the internet. The Consumer Protection (Distance Selling) Regulations 2000 provide that:

- consumers may cancel contracts within seven days and
- the contract must be performed within 30 days from the day after ordering unless otherwise agreed between the parties.

Before consumers decide to buy

You must provide consumers in advance them with the following information (for instance in a catalogue or advertisement):

- the name and address of the company (PO address is not enough)
- description of the goods
- price, including all taxes
- payment arrangements
- any delivery costs
- delivery arrangements (within 30 days of order unless agreed otherwise)
- the right to cancel the order
- how to cancel the order

- cost of using the means of any distance communication (eg premium telephone rates)
- information on any after sales service and guarantees
- the period for which the offer or price remains valid.

When consumers decide to buy

You must provide the customer with this information in **writing**, no later than **by the time the goods are delivered**. (Information regarding how long the offer or price remains valid does not need to be in writing).

The information must be provided clearly and in a way which is appropriate. For this purpose, e-mail may be sufficient where the customer has placed the order by e-mail. Where a supplier fails to give a consumer the required information in good time, the contract is unenforceable against the consumer.

Cancelling orders

Consumers have a right to cancel orders within seven working days without giving any reason and without penalty. Time starts from the day the goods are received or, if later, the date when written confirmation was received. The right to cancel also allows the customer to cancel any related credit agreement. A retailer's failure to provide customers with written confirmation about the right to cancel is a criminal offence punishable by a fine.

Where a customer exercises the right to cancel, the seller must refund the money as soon as possible and, at the latest, within 30 days of receiving a written notice of the customer's decision to cancel. The seller may charge for the cost of return post. A failure to repay the customer within 30 days may be a criminal offence.

Certain contracts are excluded from the right to cancel – for example, goods made to a customer's specification. There are also items which cannot be returned such as sealed computer software which has been opened, newspapers and flowers – unless you have agreed otherwise.

 WARNING: You cannot contract out of the Consumer Protection (Distance Selling) Regulations 2000.

Despite the regulations, in 2000, the Office of Fair Trading carried out a 'sweep' of 637 UK websites offering to sell goods or services. This found

that 52% failed to give easily accessible information on refund or exchange policies and how they would handle consumer's personal details.

You have been warned!

Terms and conditions in customer contracts

What was said earlier about terms and conditions applies equally to contracts with customers. Some traders want to protect themselves by having at least some simple terms. This is fine, so long as the terms are 'incorporated' at or before the contract is made. It is no good making a contract, agreeing a price, arranging delivery and then the salesperson saying 'Oh, these are our terms'. From the legal point of view that will be far too late

To avoid the problem about goods being 'sold' twice, a simple contract term will enable you to retain ownership until the goods have been paid for.

- The seller remains the owner of all goods until they have been paid for in full and any cheque given in payment has been cleared.

It may be that when goods are ordered you are uncertain as to the price you will have to pay your suppliers and therefore do not wish to be caught with a shortfall. Simple – have this term in your contract.

- The price to be paid is that ruling at the date of delivery.

Then there can be no argument.

Customers and manufacturers

This section is to remind you that where an aggrieved customer complains about defective goods it is up to you to put the matter right. It will not be your fault, but it is your responsibility because of the contract between you and the customer. He has no legal claim against the manufacturer because there was no contract.

There is sometimes a right to claim against a manufacturer damages for 'negligence' or for 'product liability' (see chapter 9). But this rarely arises.

Guarantees

The law relating to manufacturers' guarantees has changed. Regulation 16

of the Sale and Supply of Goods to Consumers Regulations 2002 sets out new rules when goods are sold to consumers and a guarantee is provided.

- If a guarantee is offered, it will now have contractual effect. That means that a consumer can sue the manufacturer if he fails to honour whatever he offers.
- Guarantees must be in plain, intelligible language (and, for goods sold in the UK, in English), spelling out the contents of the guarantee, how claims are to be made and how long the guarantee lasts.
- The seller (as well as the manufacturer) has to supply these details in writing or another durable medium, if requested by a consumer and the court may enforce the consumer's rights.

 WARNING: Defective goods are your problem. You cannot shirk your responsibility by fobbing the customer off and telling him to contact the manufacturer.

Stolen goods, etc.

The law of the land is very clear. A person selling something cannot pass title to it (that is, ownership of it) unless:

- he is the owner
- he is in possession with the consent of the true owner.

It follows, therefore, that where something is stolen, the thief cannot ever obtain 'title'. The item will always belong to the true owner.

Thus, should you sell goods which prove to have been stolen (even though you bought them in good faith), your customer cannot become the owner. If the true owner traces the goods and takes them back (as he is fully entitled to do) the customer has a good claim against you to which you have no defence.

Special rules about cars and hire-purchase

See chapter 6

Credit notes

From time to time you will have a customer who buys goods, and when he

gets home, decides that he does not like them. This is quite common with clothes. The customer may ask for his money back.

Many shops have a policy of always refunding money if goods come back in a pristine condition (but beware the rules about reselling 'new' goods – see page 122). However, you have no legal obligation to make a refund. If you agree to take the goods back, the most you need do is offer a credit note, to which you may add conditions about how long it is valid and for what it may be redeemed.

 WARNING: If you said that you would take goods back and refund the price at the time of the sale – that becomes a term of the contract and you are legally bound by it.

Children

There is a popular belief that children cannot make contracts. This is not the case. Young people under the age of 18 can and do make legally binding contracts for the purchase of goods of all kinds. They buy sweets and comics, books, musical items of all kinds, clothes, food and motor vehicles. Any contract for what the law calls (rather archaically) 'necessaries' is valid and binding on the child. As the vast majority of contracts are completed at one go – the child buys and pays for the goods at the same time – there are very few legal disputes.

The only time you might have difficulties is when the following coincide:

● you had supplied goods to a child which were not 'necessaries'
● the child did not pay for them … or
● you provided credit
● then you try to recover the money by legal action.

On the child's behalf it would have to be shown that the goods were so inappropriate that you, as a reasonable trader, ought to have known that they were too expensive or completely unsuitable for a person of that age.

 WARNING: Beware of selling expensive jewellery or clothing to customers who are obviously under age.

 WARNING: If you have any doubt, ask the child whether his parents know what he is buying. If there is any uncertainty ask him to come back with his Mum or Dad. That may well solve the problem for you.

 WARNING: It is a criminal offence to sell some things to children – see page 136 in Chapter 7

Uncollected goods

It is extraordinary that some people will buy goods and never take delivery of them; or they will take things for repair or servicing and never return to collect them.

For new goods being sold in your shop, the rules are set out in Chapter 5 (page 78).

When articles are left for dry-cleaning, repair or other treatment, you may deal with this in two ways.

1. Have a simple contract term in the document you hand to the customer – or a large, clearly visible notice where the customer can see it which says:

 > Goods not collected after 14 days will be sold.

2. Otherwise you will have to follow a different route set out in the Torts (Interference with Goods) Act 1977. This created two powers:

 (1) to impose on the owner an obligation to collect them when they are ready. This is done by notice in writing which specifies:

 * your name and address, and details of the goods and where they are
 * that they are ready to collect
 * how much is due to you.

 This notice may be given at any time after the goods have been repaired, treated, valued, stored, etc. It may be:

 * delivered to the customer

- left at his address … or
- sent to him by post.

(2) to give notice of your intention to sell the goods. This notice must be in writing and be sent by post (either registered or recorded delivery) setting out the same details as above adding:

- how long the customer has to collect the goods before the sale takes place. This must be a reasonable period and at least three months when you are owed money.

It would be sensible to combine these notices.

There is one point which you must understand about this power of sale. It is only available to you when you are 'reasonably satisfied' that the person who left the item 'owns the goods'.

Therefore, a child who brings in an adult's coat to be cleaned, or a man who leaves a woman's fur coat at a furrier, are at first sight not the owners. If the goods are not collected and you sell them, you may be in greater difficulty than if you had declined the custom.

This makes it even more sensible to have the notice referred to above – and always to take the name and address of the customer.

Summary of Key Learning Points

1. There is an overlap with criminal law here; you can refuse to sell something, but if it is wrongly described or priced you may be guilty of an offence – even though no one lost money or was prejudiced.

2. In commercial contracts 'terms and conditions' play a large role. Whose terms apply depends on the way the contract was made.

3. The law says that to be effective, terms and conditions must be imposed or incorporated into the contract by being drawn to the buyer's attention <u>at or before</u> the time it is made. If they are not, they have no legal effect.

4. Do <u>not</u> sign any document unless you understand the legal consequences of doing so.

5. Make sure that employees know who is empowered to make contracts.

6. You cannot contract out of the Consumer Protection (Distance Selling) Regulations 2000.

7. Make certain that staff – particularly those on commission and part-timers – do not sell any goods unless they know what they are doing.

8. Make sure that you understand when you take on responsibility for risk.

9. Defective goods are <u>your</u> problem. You cannot shirk your responsibility by fobbing the customer off and telling him to contact the manufacturer.

10. If you said that you would take goods back and refund the price at the time of the sale that becomes a term of the contract and you are legally bound by it.

11. Beware of selling expensive jewellery or clothing to customers who are obviously under age.

12. If you have any doubt ask children whether their parents know what they are buying; if there is any uncertainty ask them to come back with their Mum or Dad. That may well solve the problem for you.

13. It is a criminal offence to sell some things to children.

Checklist

☞ Does everyone (who needs to) know about the relevant Advertising Codes of Practice? Do we – and our PR people – follow them properly?

☞ Do you use telesales, or the Internet? Have you systems in place to ensure that consumers are provided with all the information required by the Distance Selling Regulations 2000?

☞ Do all managers understand the basics of contract law and how to resolve customers' complaints and disputes? Have they been trained? What do we do to keep them up to date with changes in the law?

☞ When we buy from our suppliers, are both sides clear about their rights and obligations? Do our Buyers understand contract law – and the vital importance of contract terms? What training do we give them?

☞ Do we accept special orders from our customers? If so, do all key staff understand and follow company systems about price, delivery, etc.?

☞ Do we understand how and when ownership of goods changes hands and where the risk lies? Are we protected against risks?

☞ Do we accept responsibility for defective goods? How do we handle complaints about defects and still retain our customers' goodwill?

3

Your Legal Obligations Under A Contract

Having dealt with the preliminaries we shall now look at the legal rules which apply after a contract has been made between traders and their customers.

Price

As we have seen, from a civil law standpoint there is no legal requirement for the price to be known when the contract is made. Both you and your customer know that what is being sold has to be paid for and the law assumes either that the amount is obvious or lays down rules for calculating it. (See Chapter 7 for criminal law rules.)

When existing goods are sold across the counter the price is paid there and then and will be either what is marked on the goods, or the shelf-edge or what the trader asks for. Payment is in cash, by cheque or credit-card; if the price is large, credit may come into it (see Chapter 6).

For 'future goods', which have to be ordered or manufactured, the price may be known when the order is placed – in which case that will be what the customer has to pay, even though actual payment may be delayed until the goods are ready for delivery. The parties may agree to fix the price at a later date (to take account of price increases or currency fluctuations, for example) by having a simple contract term as suggested in Chapter 2:

- The price to be paid is that ruling at the date of delivery.

 WARNING: Trying to allow for later price increases may have legal consequences under the Unfair Contract Terms Act 1977 or the Unfair Terms in Consumer Contracts Regulations 1999 (see page 62).

If there is no agreement and nothing was discussed at the time, section 8 of the Sale of Goods Act 1979 says that:

- 'the buyer must pay a reasonable price'

The joy of that helpful formula is that 'reasonable' is a word which can mean whatever you want. Lawyers use it a lot.

If there was a real dispute about what should be paid, one would look at the price for similar goods charged by rival traders. The problems that this could cause are very good reasons for making sure that the price is known and fixed when the contract is made.

 WARNING: In commercial contracts there may be a 'price variation clause' enabling a supplier to increase an agreed price between the order and delivery.

Time

There are often arguments between customer and trader about delays in delivery. The buyer expected the goods to be available within a few days; the retailer knew that there would be at least a month's wait. What does the law have to say?

Rather surprisingly to non-lawyers, the rule set out in section 10 of the Sale of Goods Act 1979 is that in ordinary contracts between retailers and customers, time is not regarded as being 'of the essence'. The goods must simply be delivered within a 'reasonable' time, and you will know by now what that means. Either party can make time 'of the essence':

- by making it a term of the contract, or
- after the contract, by giving notice that time is to run.

Making time part of the contract

When a customer orders goods, he may want them by a particular time – for example, a wedding dress *before* the vital day; a carpet for laying before the furniture arrives. If he tells you about these dates and explains how important it is that the goods arrive in time, time is then said to be 'of the essence'. If the goods arrive after the specified time or date, you are in breach of contract; the customer can refuse to take the goods at a later date and can claim compensation from you if he is put to additional expense.

To avoid problems, you and the customer should ensure that the date is written down on any invoice or contract document.

Giving notice that time is running

Often, when there is no previous agreement, so that time is not running, the customer gets fed up. Each time he asks he is told that there are delays at the factory, or with the importer. At last his patience runs out and he wants to bring the contract to an end.

He is perfectly within his rights to write to you saying:

'Deliver the goods I have ordered within (say) 14 days, or the deal is off and I want my money back.'

The only way to avoid these problems is to have a contract term which says:

● The seller will do its best to meet any suggested delivery date, but it is not bound to deliver by any specified date and neither party may give notice to make time of the essence.

 WARNING: Trying to avoid time running may have legal consequences under the Unfair Contract Terms Act 1977 or the Unfair Terms in Consumer Contracts Regulations 1999 (see Chapter 4)

Terms implied under the Sale of Goods Act 1979

An important preliminary term which arises under section 12 of the Act is that you have a right to sell the goods in your shop – in other words, that you are lawfully in possession of them and, if they still belong to someone else (see 'retention of title', Chapter 4) you are selling them with the true owner's knowledge and consent.

For all retailers, there are three extremely important terms which automatically appear in every contract for the sale of goods. In the contracts you make with your customers you are not allowed to exclude the terms. The people who supply you, on the other hand, may have 'exclusion clauses' in their contracts which limit or avoid the impact of these terms (that is one of the reasons why it is so important for you to understand how a contract is made and whose terms take precedence). The good news is that you can challenge such 'exclusion clauses' by reference to the Unfair Contract Terms Act 1977, which says that they will only be upheld if they are 'fair and reasonable'. And the onus of proving that they are rests on the supplier – who may find it extremely hard to justify his own small print.

The three terms are called 'implied terms' because they arise automatically; they do not have to be written down or specially mentioned when you are negotiating with your customer. The law just says the terms are there, willy-nilly.

In many ways they are the most important part of what is known as 'consumer law'. The three terms concern description, quality and fitness for use.

The implied term of description

Section 13 of the Sale of Goods Act 1979 says:

● Where there is a contract for sale by description there is an implied term that the goods will correspond with the description.

Unlike the other two (as we shall see) this term applies to all contracts for the sale of goods – private sales as well as those by retailers. This means that anyone who wants to sell a car or surplus household items must be extremely careful not to make claims about them which are not accurate, a common error being to say that a car is in excellent condition when really it has serious shortcomings. One of the few cases which deal with this term (*Beale v Taylor, (1967)*) concerned the private sale of a car.

As far as traders are concerned, the word 'description' has a wide meaning and covers not only such obvious things as a brand name or make or colour but also statements like 'in first-class condition' or 'nearly new' when second-hand goods are being sold.

Sometimes there is an argument about whether there was any description because the shopper simply saw an article and offered to buy it. 'Description' means more than what anyone says. It extends to the packaging, labelling and any publicity material which the would-be buyer might have seen that might have induced him to think about buying the item.

The position is not altered merely because the customer selects goods himself in a supermarket or self-service shop.

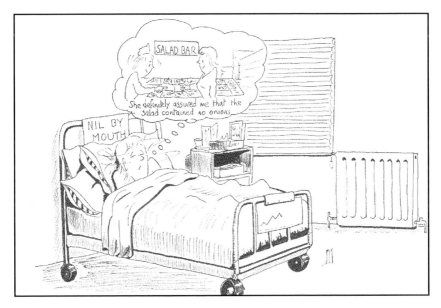

Where what is being sold is 'future goods', there must, almost by definition, have been a description. In order to let the customer know what was available you would have listed in detail the size, pattern, fabric etc – all the items which he needed to know to make his choice and which you required to place an order with your manufacturer or supplier. The customer would have relied on what was said to him.

Again it is worth reminding readers of the need to be so careful when answering customers' questions. In 1995 a supermarket assistant was asked whether a salad contained onion. Not knowing whether it did or not, she said 'no'. In fact it did. The customer bought it and was violently ill because he was allergic to onions. If she had said she did not know, the assistant would not have implicated the supermarket.

 WARNING: Make staff realise the importance of knowledge and accuracy – and of saying 'I don't know' when appropriate.

Section 15 of the Act also says:

● If the sale is a sale by sample as well as by description it is not sufficient that the bulk of the goods correspond with the sample if the goods do not also correspond with the sample.

Customers may have very different views about this than the hapless retailer. A roll of wallpaper or a tin of paint may differ in shade from a supposedly identical sample. You will say that this is inevitable because one batch can never be guaranteed to be exactly the same as another.

If something does not match its description, the customer has the right to reject it and claim his money back (see Chapter 12). This applies equally when the bulk is not the same as the sample – it all goes back – subject to a new right of 'partial rejection' (see Chapter 5).

Overlap with civil and criminal law

You must bear in mind that what we have been talking about here is the way the civil law affects goods. Remember that there are quite separate criminal law rules about description, with quite different sanctions, which will be outlined in a later chapter.

Sales 'in the course of a business'

The Sale of Goods Act says that the terms about quality and fitness are found where the seller:

- sells goods in the course of a business

This means the sale of any goods in the course of any business. It will therefore cover not only the sort of thing you commonly sell but anything else – a furniture shop selling a salesman's car, a solicitor selling a computer. These are all sales 'in the course of a business'. For example, in 1981 a shoe repairer sold in his shop an electric fire of his own. The fire did not comply with safety regulations. The court held he was liable and he was convicted of a criminal charge. But he would have had no defence to a civil claim for breach of description.

The implied term of satisfactory quality

In 1994, substantial changes were made to the law of sale of goods which took effect on 3 January 1995. The Sale and Supply of Goods Act 1994 introduced a new term of 'satisfactory' quality by amending section 14 of the Sale of Goods Act 1979. (All references to the 1979 Act mean that Act in its amended wording.)

Section 14(2) says:

● Where the seller sells goods in the course of a business there is an implied term that the goods are of satisfactory quality

This applies to all contracts, as we have seen, and applies to all kinds of goods. The words 'satisfactory quality' are new, replacing the familiar phrase – 'merchantable' quality – which had been used for hundreds of years. In 1987, a report by the reforming Law Commissions used the word 'acceptable' to define quality but when an amending Bill was brought to Parliament in 1994 it was decided that 'satisfactory' was better because something that was 'acceptable' – like a car with a dent in the bodywork – might not be satisfactory, because buyers expect products to be as near perfect as possible.

Section 14(2A) then contains a definition of this new concept of quality.

● … goods are of satisfactory quality if they meet the standard that a reasonable person would regard as satisfactory, taking account of any description of the goods, the price (if relevant) and all the other relevant circumstances.

In order to be able to assess whether goods meet the definition, one has to look at everything about them, including the price, which suggests that if a very low price is paid for an article it may be that the mythical 'reasonable' person might think that the quality might be lower than normal.

Another new feature is section 14(2B) of the Act where there is a non-exhaustive list of 'ingredients' to be taken into consideration when measuring how satisfactory goods are:

● … the quality of goods includes their state and condition and the following (among others) are in appropriate cases aspects of the quality of goods –

 (a) fitness for the purpose for which goods of the kind in question are commonly supplied,

 WARNING: If you fail to indicate that goods are NOT fit for all their common purposes you may be in breach of the quality term if you sell something normally supplied for two purposes but which is actually only fit for one.

(b) appearance and finish,

 WARNING: What a customer eventually receives must not be different from what he saw in a showroom when he was placing his order.

(c) freedom from minor defects,

 WARNING: These are separate categories. A customer is entitled to expect goods not only to look right but may reject them if there is a minor fault – even though that can be easily remedied.

(d) safety,

 WARNING: Goods should meet any standards or regulations dealing with stability, flame-proofing, the removal of sharp edges and risks of being trapped – and should avoid the sort of carelessness that results in nails being exposed.

 WARNING: Take care not to infringe the General Safety Requirement in section 10 Consumer Protection Act 1987 (see Chapter 8)

(e) durability.

 WARNING: Goods are expected to last for a reasonable time; the requirement takes effect at the time of supply.

Although it is recognised that how long goods will last depends on the way they are treated, customers have a view – often rather inflated – of the life expectancy of the more expensive items they buy. They may have been encouraged by advertisements claiming that a product has been 'tested to destruction' or has been shown to 'last 10 years in normal use'. There may also be reference to a guarantee or warranty for a particular period which, again, may make a customer believe that what he is going to buy will last that long.

 WARNING: The implied term of satisfactory quality applies to second-hand goods as well as new ones.

Important exceptions

Section 14(2C) contains two very important exceptions which can be of considerable benefit to retailers. It says that the promise of satisfactory quality does not extend to any matter:

- specifically drawn to the buyer's attention before the contract is made
- where the buyer examines the goods before the contract is made, which that examination ought to reveal.

If properly used, these two provisos can give you a great deal of help. The first one uses the word 'specifically'. This means that, if you want to use the law quite properly to avoid liability, whatever is wrong must be itemised and clearly told to the customer. Merely saying 'seconds' or 'shop-soiled' will not protect you against claims that the goods were chipped or broken or never used. List faults accurately on a label securely attached to the article and – better safe than sorry – also write them down on the sales invoice.

The second proviso will only apply if the buyer actually examines the goods; and only then if you can show that what he is complaining about would or should have come to light while he was making the examination. A cursory look would not be sufficient unless it can be shown that it would have revealed, for example, that a wheel was missing from a car.

Take the sale of a used car. If the would-be buyer has it inspected by a vehicle-examiner, and the brakes fail shortly afterwards, you could argue that the test ought to have spotted that there was a worn brake pipe. If you succeed, the customer has no claim against you.

 WARNING: Beware of customers who buy 'blind'. You can never rely on the second proviso in that case.

It is vitally important that you understand that these provisos apply to information given to customers, or examinations made by them, before the contract is made.

 WARNING: It is no good telling someone as he leaves the shop that there is something wrong with the goods. That is too late. The first proviso will not apply.

There is also a 'get out' proviso where the goods are bought in a sale by sample. Section 14(2C)(c) says that there is no promise of satisfactory quality

● which would have been apparent on a reasonable examination of the sample

and this applies even if the buyer does not in fact examine the sample.

Because this definition is new, it will mean that we will have to wait and see how judges react when cases come before them. It will also mean that the body of legal understanding which built up when 'merchantable quality' was the basis of a dispute will no longer be very relevant – although the long line of cases may still be a help in trying to predict what should happen.

Public statements

The Sale and Supply of Goods to Consumers Regulations 2002 (see below page 93) added another factor to be taken into accounts when measuring whether goods are of satisfactory quality.

A new section 14(2D) to the Sale of Goods Act 1979 says that the court is to have regard to any 'public statements' on specific characteristics of the goods made by the seller or the producer (which really means the manufacturer) or his representative in advertising or labelling. This would bring before the court the sort of things which one finds in adverts where manufacturers make promises about the durability or strength or suitability of their products. One can think of floor coverings bearing claims that they are 'guaranteed for ten years' – until now worthless puff – but which can be relied on by a consumer.

This new term will not apply in three cases:

● if the seller can show that at the time the contract was made, he had no knowledge of the statement;

● that the statement had been withdrawn before the contract was made – or anything misleading or incorrect had been put right;

- that the decision to buy could not have been influenced by the statement. Remember, the onus will be on the seller to prove this.

The implied term of fitness for use

Section 14(3) of the Sale of Goods Act 1979 contains the third implied term, which is not significantly changed by the amending Act in 1994. Let us look at the main part (I have cut out reference to 'credit-brokers' – that will be dealt with later in Chapter 6).

- Where … the buyer, expressly or by implication, makes known to the seller any particular purpose for which the goods are being bought, there is an implied term that the goods … are reasonably fit for that purpose, whether or not that is a purpose for which such goods are commonly supplied, except where the circumstances show that the buyer does not rely, or that it is unreasonable for him to rely on the skill or judgment of the seller …

The first two lines mean that the customer can either tell you what he wants to do with a product: e.g. 'I want to put this carpet in my living room' or 'Can I use this paint in a bathroom?' It is also the case that goods must be able to perform their obvious function – a fridge must keep food cold; a kettle must boil water; glue must actually stick things together. Or, by saying nothing and just choosing an item, he indicates the intended use – by selecting a screw-driver, it is understood that the customer wants to insert or remove screws.

Product knowledge assumed

It is now generally assumed that professionals who sell things will know more about their main characteristics than the man or woman in the street who comes into the shop. There is a burden placed on you as a retailer either to be skilled and knowledgeable about the whole range of products that you sell or to make it quite plain that you have no specialised know-how, something which a court might find improbable.

Go back to the carpet. The customer has told you where he wants to lay this particular carpet – in his living room. It may have caught his eye because of a low price but it may be an inferior quality one, or excellent for a spare room.

The skilled retailer will get talking to the customer, find out where he lives, how many people live in the house – a carpet will react very differently to use by a widow living alone than a young couple with three small children, a dog and two cats.

When the customer has given you lots of clues about his plans, if you allow him to buy the wrong carpet, because you are desperate for a sale or do not care what happens afterwards, you will be in breach of the Sale of Goods Act.

Again, consider the screw-driver. The obvious purpose is to screw screws – but anyone who has done any DIY will know that you can use screw-drivers to open tins of paint, prise up floor-boards and prop up doors while hanging them. If a customer asks you whether a screw-driver is strong enough to use as a lever, be extremely careful before you reply. If you say 'yes' and the customer tries to open a tin and a piece of metal flies off and makes him blind in one eye you would be liable, not only for the price of the tool but for the thousands of pounds compensation for blindness.

A common complaint in furniture retailing is that a chair or table broke when someone stood on it to change a light-bulb. Of course the immediate response is that that is not 'a purpose for which such goods are commonly supplied' – but it is widely known that people will do daft things. If you are selling furniture you would do yourself a favour by preventing complaints, as well as discouraging legal action, by reminding customers that they should treat what they buy properly and with care.

 WARNING: You will be liable for what you sell unless you can show that the shopper insisted on buying something inappropriate against your advice and guidance.

Sales and second-hand goods

There is nothing wrong in having sales. The main thing is to make sure you comply with the rules about how price reductions are shown (see Chapter 7). Other than that, the legal situation is exactly the same as when you sell ordinary stock. The normal rules about the need to meet the standard of quality apply.

However, for 'seconds' the situation may be different. Looking at the definition of 'satisfactory quality' in section 14(2A), it says that the reasonable person would take account of any description, the price and all

other relevant circumstances. It must be the case that marking items as 'seconds' is part of the description which indicates to the would-be shopper that they are reduced in price for some reason. It must be 'relevant' that the price is lower. Although the goods must still do what most people would expect them to do, it must be obvious (at least to a 'reasonable person') that they are not in the same condition as brand new goods.

For good measure, it would be prudent to say in what way they may be inferior to first-quality goods. In that way, even if there is a legal challenge, you can rely on the proviso in section 14(2C)(a) which does away with any promise of quality for 'any matter making goods unsatisfactory specifically drawn to the buyer's attention before the contract is made'.

There is a general presumption that what is sold by retail is new; second-hand goods so described are obviously not new. They must have been owned by someone else before you mark them in that way. Again, a reasonable person will be put on his guard that anything described as 'second-hand' or 'used' may have had a previous owner about whom very little will be known.

'Special purchase' is a description frequently to be found in shops, particularly during sales. Such goods must be new; they must meet all the tests for 'satisfactory quality' and should not be inferior in any way. Nor should they be shown with price reductions (see Chapter 7).

Summary of Key Learning Points

1. Trying to allow for later price increases may have legal consequences under the Unfair Contract Terms Act 1977 or the Unfair Terms in Consumer Contracts Regulations 1994.

2. In commercial contracts there may be a 'price variation clause' enabling a supplier to increase an agreed price between the order and delivery.

3. Trying to avoid time running may have legal consequences under the Unfair Contract Terms Act 1977 or the Unfair Terms in Consumer Contracts Regulations 1994 (see Chapter 4).

4. Make staff realise the importance of knowledge and accuracy – and of saying 'I don't know' when appropriate.

5. If you fail to indicate that goods are <u>not</u> fit for all their common purposes you may be in breach of the quality term if you sell something normally supplied for two purposes but which is actually only fit for one.

6. These are separate categories. A customer is entitled to expect goods not only to look right but may reject them if there is a minor fault – <u>even though</u> that can be easily remedied.

7. Take care not to infringe the General Safety Requirement in section 10, Consumer Protection Act 1987 (see Chapter 8).

8. Goods are expected to last for a reasonable time; the requirement takes effect at the time of supply.

9. The implied term of satisfactory quality applies to second-hand goods as well as new ones.

10. Beware of customers who buy 'blind'. You can never rely on the second proviso in that case.

11. It is no good telling someone as he leaves the shop that there is something wrong with the goods. That is too late. The first proviso will not apply.

12. You will be liable for what you sell unless you can show that the shopper insisted on buying something inappropriate against your advice and guidance.

Checklist

☞ How do we handle future price increases? Do we pass them on or build them in to the present price?

☞ What are we doing to protect ourselves against problems when goods are slow in coming from the suppliers?

☞ Have all our sales staff received detailed training in product knowledge? Do they clearly understand what to say to a customer when they do not know the answer to a question?

☞ When talking to customers about what they are thinking of buying, do our sales staff understand the importance of:

 • fitness for purpose?
 • appearance and finish?
 • freedom from defects?
 • safety?
 • durability?

☞ What training do we give them on these aspects – and on product knowledge generally?

☞ Do sales staff understand what they say to customers asking about goods which are reduced or bought in for sales?

☞ What have you done to find out about statements made about goods by their manufactureres or importers in adverts, publicity material?

4

Working Through A Contract

We have seen in the previous chapter that you, as a retailer, have certain obligations which arise simply by making a contract for the sale of goods. There is nothing you can do to prevent these terms applying to the contract; the law says that they do. Many trade sectors have complicated and lengthy small print which is intended to avoid or limit the extent of legal duties. In commercial contracts for the sale of goods, these terms can be modified which can lead to an imbalance between your rights against your supplier and the customer's claim against you.

Consumer sales

The rights given to private individuals as customers set out in sections 13, 14 and 15 of the Sale of Goods Act 1979 are 'inalienable' – they cannot be excluded or modified. Rather confusingly, the legal provision which explains this is not in the 1979 Act but in section 6(2) of the Unfair Contract Terms Act 1977:

- As against a person dealing as consumer, liability for breach of the obligations arising from:
 (a) section 13, 14 or 15 of the 1979 Act
 (b) section 9,10 or 11 of the (Supply of Goods (Implied Terms) Act 1973) – (which apply to hire-purchase contracts – see Chapter 6) cannot be excluded or restricted by reference to any contract term.

This means what it says. So any contract term, whether it contains formal phrases like 'all conditions arising by statute or otherwise are expressly excluded' or colloquial words like 'no warranty given' or 'sold as seen' has no legal effect. The words may be on the piece of paper but the law ignores them.

In addition, it is a criminal offence under the Consumer Transactions (Restrictions on Statements) Order 1976 to have such a term in a contract or to display any sign which suggests that you will not deal with complaints which arise from a breach of your obligations under the Sale of Goods Act.

 WARNING: Do not put up notices which say 'no money back' or 'no refunds' or 'sale goods not taken back'

 WARNING: Do not have any contract term which says 'no warranty given' or 'sold as seen' or which tries to limit or avoid liability under the 1979 Act.

There have been a number of cases in which a person who is a trader has still been treated as 'dealing as consumer' – which means that the terms would have no effect. For example, a company buying a motor boat (*Rasbora v. J C L Marine (1977)*); a company buying a car for a director (*R & B Customs Brokers Co Ltd v. UDT (1980)*). One could argue that a solicitor buying a carpet for his office would also be a 'consumer'.

These legal decisions may no longer apply. Under the Sale and Supply of Goods to Consumers Regulations 2002, 'consumer' is defined as 'a natural person who is acting for purposes which are outside his trade, business or profession'. This means, for example, that a self-employed lawyer who buys a laptop for use at work and at home is not covered under these rules, though he almost certainly would have been under the previous law described above.

Maddeningly, the definition of 'consumer' is not carried forward into the 1979 Act – so one has to look in at least two places to see what is what.

Contracts between you and your suppliers

The law concerning commercial contracts is quite different. The use of exclusion clauses which limit or avoid liability under sections 13, 14 and 15 of the Sale of Goods Act 1979 (dealing with description and quality) is allowed. Your rights are not inalienable. For many years this caused great unfairness, because retailers had to refund customers but were prevented from claiming anything from the real culprits, the manufacturers, who hedged themselves with very effective small print.

However, the Unfair Contract Terms Act 1977 does give some

assistance to traders. Although these 'exclusion clauses' are allowed, section 6(3) of the Act says:

- As against a person dealing otherwise than as consumer, the liability....can be excluded or restricted by reference to a contract term, but only in so far as the term satisfies the requirement of reasonableness.

The 'reasonableness test' is looked at a few paragraphs below.

Other terms where the Unfair Contract Terms Act may help

The Act applies not only to contracts for the sale of goods but to the supply of services, like car-hire, leasing agreements, carriage and transport of goods, garages servicing, rail and air travel, the supply of gas and electricity and telephones. You may challenge any contract containing terms like the following:

- Vague delivery dates – 'Any date given is a guide only and the seller is not obliged to deliver at any time' – which also state that time is not of the essence
- Delivery clauses which allow manufacturers to supply goods either very early – Christmas stock arriving in July – or very late, not only without penalty but still requiring you to pay in full on receipt of invoice
- Deviation – when the supplier's terms allow him to supply something different from what you order. These may be in terms of quantity (e.g. more or less than the order) or the nature of the goods themselves (sending rackets for tennis instead of squash, for instance).

Section 3 of the Act applies when you, as a trader, have to deal with another trader on his 'written standard terms of business'. It says that the supplier cannot by a contract term:

(a) when himself in breach of contract, exclude or restrict any liability of his in respect of the breach; or

(b) claim to be entitled:

 (i) to render a contractual performance substantially different from that which was reasonably expected of him, or

(ii) in respect of the whole or any part of his contractual obligation, to render no performance at all,

except in so far as … the term satisfies the requirement of reasonableness.

In each of the three examples above, you can argue that the supplier is trying to give himself the opportunity of not meeting his obligations – either in part or at all. A court might well find that a term that allows delivery to be delayed almost indefinitely is really a 'claim to be entitled not to perform the contract at all' and ignore it. Similarly with 'deviation' clauses.

The section also outlaws a term which allows a supplier to break his contract and then refuse to compensate the victim.

The 'test of reasonableness'

When deciding whether a contract term is fair, the court will look at section 11 of the Unfair Contract Terms Act 1977 which says:

- The term shall have been a fair and reasonable one to be included having regard to the circumstances which were, or ought reasonably to have been, known to or in the contemplation of the parties when the contract was made.

This means that hindsight will not help you. You have to look at the picture known to both sides when the contract was negotiated.

The Act also contains a list of factors which shall also be taken into account when judging fairness. These are set out in the Second Schedule to the 1977 Act and include the following points:

1 the relative bargaining strength of the parties, taking into account alternative sources of supply
2 whether you as buyer received an inducement to agree to the term, or could have made a different contract with other people without such a term
3 whether you knew of the term, or ought to have known, given the custom in the trade and any previous dealing with the supplier
4 where the term restricts liability if some condition is not complied with, whether it was reasonably practical at the time of the contract to expect compliance with it

5 whether the goods were specially manufactured, processed or adapted for the customer.

Looking at the reasonableness test and these five guidelines, it is frequently very difficult for any large company to convince a court that limiting or avoiding its liability, or breaking its contract without penalty, is 'reasonable' when it is dealing with a small High Street retailer.

Incidentally, section 11(4) says that if a supplier tries to limit liability by reference to a sum of money, when the test of reasonableness is applied, the court will also look at:

- the resources available to meet the liability
- whether insurance was available.

In 1994 there was a case about the supply of computer software. A local authority suffered a loss of £1.3 million, but the supplier limited its liability to £100,000. The court held that the supplier, which was a giant multi-national company carrying insurance for £50 million, should carry the full loss (*St Albans City Council v. International Computers Ltd*).

Onus of proof

Finally, one of the most important aspects of the Unfair Contract Terms Act is that it places the burden of proof on the person relying on the term. This means that you challenge what is in the small print but the other side has to justify what may well be an indefensible legal position.

Terms outside the 1977 Act

There are still many terms which are repugnant to most retailers but which are not covered by the Act. For example:

- *minimum quantity orders* where the contract says that you have to place an order for at least £x worth of goods

- *price variation clauses*, which allow the manufacturer to increase the price between order and delivery; and also, by reference to some formula, permit an increase even after delivery and payment.

- *title retention clauses* – these are devices used by manufacturers and suppliers to retain 'title' (that is, legal ownership) of goods at all times up to actual payment. The hope is that they will be

protected by remaining as owners if you, their customer, go into liquidation or become bankrupt. If this happens, all they need to do then is pick up the goods and take them away.

Normally, when a business fails, the unsold stock is one asset that the receiver, liquidator or trustee-in-bankruptcy can seize and sell; the money produced goes towards paying the creditors in the statutory order.

Where title is retained, however, the liquidator has no claim; he cannot hold on to the goods, he must let the true owner take them back. No one else has any claim against the goods either.

 WARNING: Remember that goods subject to 'title retention' do not belong to you; they cannot be used as security for credit, overdrafts, etc.

Indemnity clauses

Many contracts contain clauses by which party A tries to make party B indemnify A against the consequences of A's own breach of contract or failure to perform the contract properly.

For contracts made by consumers (or, more accurately, by people 'dealing as consumers' – which may be rather wider than the private individual), such indemnity clauses will only be acceptable if they meet the 'reasonableness test'. Many of those commonly found in contracts of carriage by sea or in car-hire would be struck down because they are caught by section 4 of the Unfair Contract Terms Act 1977.

However, no other type of indemnifier is protected. It is possible, therefore, that a manufacturer of goods which turn out to be faulty could relieve himself of liability to you the retailer (and to whom he would otherwise be liable under sections 13 or 14 of the Sale of Goods Act 1979) by inserting an indemnity clause in his contract with you. Where the faulty goods caused death or injury, the effect of such an indemnity clause could leave you without any remedy against the supplier but with full liability to the injured victim or his family.

Unfair Terms in Consumer Contracts Regulations 1999

These rules replace those introduced in 1994 and apply to virtually all contracts made with consumers which are not individually negotiated – in

other words where a consumer deals with a trader on the trader's written terms of business.

The main points of the regulations are:

- Contracts must be in 'plain, intelligible language';
- They do not apply to the main purpose of the contract or to the price;
- An 'unfair term' is one which, contrary to the requirement of 'good faith', is loaded against the consumer;
- 'Unfairness' is judged against:
 - the type of goods or services
 - all circumstances when the contract was made
 - all the terms of the contract
 - the terms of any dependent contract.
- 'Good faith' shall be measured against:
 - the parties' bargaining strength
 - any inducement to the consumer to accept the term
 - whether goods or services were supplied to consumer's special order
 - the extent to which the trader had dealt fairly and equitably with the consumer.
- A term found 'unfair' shall not bind the consumer;
- The contract will continue without the unfair term (if that is possible);
- Any ambiguous terms will be interpreted in favour of the consumer.

Schedule 3 to the Regulations contains a page and a half of examples of terms which are likely to be considered 'unfair' and include clauses which:

- exclude or limit liability for death or injury caused by negligence
- limit the consumer's rights if the trader is in breach or fails to perform all or part of the contract
- allow trader to keep deposits when consumer cancels without allowing for compensation if trader breaks the contract
- allow trader to cancel arbitrarily
- allow trader to cancel a long-term contract without notice
- automatically extend fixed-term contract where consumer does not say he wants to cancel

- allow unilateral variation without good reason
- allow price to be fixed at date of delivery or permit later price increase without giving consumer option to cancel
- require consumer to fulfil his obligations although trader in breach
- lay down compulsory arbitration or impose burden of proof on consumer.

For the first time in the UK, someone is now to be responsible for complaints about unfair contract terms. Hitherto, one had to contemplate either taking legal action oneself or, if one's complaints were rejected, risk being sued by a trader who imposed unreasonable terms.

The new regulations empower the Director General of Fair Trading to do various things. He may:

- look at complaints about unfair contract terms
- go to court for an 'injunction' to ban the use of such terms
- ask traders to give undertakings to stop using unfair terms.

The Director General issues regular Bulletins which describe the way the Office of Fair Trading looks at unfair terms in consumer contracts. A large number of contracts have been scrapped or re-written as a result of the OFT's investigations. Everyone who has anything to do with drafting any sort of contract to obtain copies of the Bulletins from: E C Logistics, Swallowfield Way, Hayes, Middlesex UB3 1DQ – tel: 0870 60 60 321; fax: 0870 60 70 321 or e-mail: oft@eclogistics.co.uk

After the contract

The main obligation on a retailer is to ensure that the goods are made available to the customer. The legal jargon is 'delivery' – which rather unhelpfully does not mean putting an item in a van to take to the customer but the transfer of possession (remember that in most cases actual ownership transferred at the instant the contract was made).

Section 28 of the Sale of Goods Act 1979 deals with the question of payment by the customer. It says:

- Unless otherwise agreed, delivery of the goods to the buyer and payment of the price are concurrent obligations.

The retailer must be able to give possession of what is being sold to the

customer who, at the same time, hands over the money. Of course there may be all sorts of variations on this simple proposition – the most obvious is where there is credit. You may be happy to let the customer take the goods away on approval or because you trust him to return and pay later.

The contract which you make with the customer may contain terms about delivery. If nothing has been agreed – and that is the general rule for the majority of retail sales – section 29 of the Sale of Goods Act 1979 lays down some principles.

- The place of delivery is your place of business.
- If you are to make delivery, you must do so within a reasonable time.
- If the goods are with someone else, there is no delivery until that person acknowledges to the customer that he is holding them.
- You must meet the cost of putting the goods into a deliverable state.

The last point is of relevance where the goods have to be assembled or the trader has to carry out checks or servicing or some formality (as with registering and doing a pre-delivery inspection on a car) before the goods are handed over. If the work is onerous or expensive, and you want to be paid, do ensure that the contract spells it out.

Lien

Anyone who is owed money and is holding someone else's property is entitled to retain it until he is paid. This is called the right of 'lien'. It is a right to keep something as security for payment. The commonest example is taking a car to a garage for servicing; when the bill is presented the motorist does not have enough money to pay. The garage is fully within its rights to keep the car until the bill is settled.

As we have seen, in the case of the sale of goods in a shop, delivery and payment are 'concurrent' events. For new goods, if the customer turns up and is unable to pay what is outstanding, you are perfectly justified in refusing to let the goods off your premises. You are exercising your lien.

 WARNING: The right to lien is lost if you part with the goods; once they have left the shop you cannot take them back.

Note that for new goods you may have retained title; if so, should the customer's cheque bounce or if he does not come back to pay the balance, you can recover the goods (assuming you can get access to them) because they are still yours. This has nothing to do with lien.

WARNING: Don't confuse 'lien' with rights of ownership.

Carriage

Normally in the case of 'specific goods' delivery – exchanging the goods for the price – takes place at your premises. Whether or not you arrange to take the goods to the customer's house depends on what you have agreed. Many bulky items will be delivered, especially 'future goods' which may even arrive directly at the customer's premises from the factory.

Whether carriage has to be paid for also depends on what was agreed at the time the contract was made. It is quite possible for a separate, later arrangement to be made when the customer realises that he cannot fit what he has bought into the boot of his car or cannot arrange to pick it up. Making a charge is perfectly normal.

What happens if you use a carrier, rather than your own transport? Assuming the customer knows about it and has agreed in principle (and unless anything else has been agreed) there is a rule in section 32 of the Sale of Goods Act 1979:

- … delivery of goods to a carrier (whether named by the buyer or not) for the purpose of transmission to the buyer is prima facie deemed to be a delivery of the goods to the buyer.

This is important because it is an aspect of 'risk' (see page 34). The law says that risk 'passes with property'. For any existing goods the ownership changed hands when the contract was made – and so did risk. For 'future goods' ownership passed when they were 'appropriated to the contract' and this might well be the moment when they were loaded on to a vehicle for delivery.

For most purposes, by the time goods are in the care of a carrier, risk (as well as ownership) has passed to the customer. If the carrier has an accident or the goods are lost in transit or stolen from the vehicle, the loss

does not fall on the retailer but on the customer, because he is the owner.

The Act goes on to impose a duty on the trader to ensure that the contract of carriage is appropriate; section 32(2) says:

● Unless otherwise authorised by the buyer, the seller must make such contract with the carrier on behalf of the buyer as may be reasonable having regard to the nature of the goods and the other circumstances of the case; and if the seller omits to do so and the goods are lost or damaged in course of transit, the buyer may decline to treat the delivery to the carrier as delivery to himself or may hold the seller responsible in damages.

A contract of carriage?

The effect of this is twofold.

First, you must ensure that the method of carriage is suitable for the goods – much more care need be taken of glassware or a computer or washing machine than a sack of seed potatoes. Proper packaging and protection are essential. Sending valuables like jewellery would need adequate recompense for loss.

Secondly, you should look at the small print of the carrier's contract to see whether it is as restrictive as is usually the case. Many carriers limit liability to a fraction of the real value of the goods or by reference to their

weight and demand that claims are made within a short period of time. Many such terms were regarded as 'unreasonable' under the old law; now, since the Unfair Terms in Consumer Contracts Regulations 1999, (see page 62) they are likely to be struck out (first, because they will not be in 'plain, legible language' and secondly because they are 'unfair').

 WARNING: *If you choose a carrier, you may be liable should anything go wrong.*

So, for many years, these rules just described applied to all contracts. They still apply to your contracts with suppliers.

However, the law has changed for consumer sales. The Sale and Supply of Goods to Consumers Regulations 2002 (see below page 93) amended section 32 of the Sale of Goods Act 1979. Now, goods in a consumer sale, where the seller is authorised or required to send goods to a consumer, delivery to a carrier is NOT delivery to the consumer.

This means that goods remain at your risk (see above, page 34) and your property until they have been delivered to the consumer.

 WARNING: *Make sure that you have adequate insurance to cover you should anything happen to goods before they are delivered to the consumer.*

 WARNING: *If you arrange carriage for a customer, that contract will be a 'consumer' one even though you and the carrier are both commercial people. For legal purposes, you are the customer's agent.*

Contracts for services

So far we have looked at contracts for the sale of goods – that is, when you, a retailer, sell items in your shop or take orders for later delivery when the goods have been manufactured.

There is another type of contract, which is very common; one for the 'supply of services'. Services covers a huge range of things. Here are a few examples:

- having a carpet laid
- servicing a car
- shoe repairs or dry-cleaning
- travel by bus, train or plane

- hiring a car
- chimney sweeping
- buying a package holiday.

This sort of arrangement includes what lawyers call contracts for 'work and materials' – that is:

- when one employs a builder to add an extension to the house
- hiring a decorator to supply and hang wallpaper
- a plumber installing a central heating system
- having a kitchen fitted.

Once upon a time, there was a discrepancy between the law of sale of goods and that covering services. Buying goods across the counter gave one all the protection of the Sale of Goods Act with the implied terms, etc. But where exactly the same goods were bought by a tradesman in the course of a 'work and materials' contract, who then added them to one's house, car, etc. the consumer had no legal rights, or at any rate none that were easy to define and quantify.

The inconsistency was removed by the Supply of Goods and Services Act 1982. Section 3(2) of that Act says that in contracts for the transfer of goods (other than a sale of goods):

- … there is an implied term that the goods will correspond with (any) description.

To bring the law on services directly into line with the new law for sale of goods, section 4(2) onwards of the Supply of Goods and Services Act 1982 imposes a standard of quality. It says:

- … there is an implied term that the goods are of a satisfactory quality.

It goes on to set out exactly the same tests as we have looked at for section 14 of the Sale of Goods Act 1979 (see Chapter 3) by inserting:

- … goods are of a satisfactory quality if they meet the standard that a reasonable person would regard as satisfactory, taking account of any description, … the price (if relevant) and all the other relevant circumstances.

To complete the picture, section 18 of the Supply of Goods and Services

Act 1982 contains a definition of 'satisfactory quality', listing the 'ingredients' fitness for purpose, appearance and finish and so on, which are described above on page 48.

Having given the customer these new rights, an amendment was made to the Unfair Contract Terms Act 1977 to bring that Act into line with the ban on exclusion clauses in straight sale of goods contracts. Section 7 of the 1977 Act says:

(1) Where the possession or ownership of goods passes under ... a contract (for services) ...

(2) As against a person dealing as consumer, liability in respect of the goods' correspondence with description or sample, or their quality or fitness for any particular purpose, cannot be excluded or restricted by reference to any such term.

 WARNING: In commercial contracts for the supply of services, limitation of these implied terms is allowed, to the extent that the exclusion is 'fair and reasonable'.

For the 'reasonableness test' see page 63.

Other important terms in service contracts

Part II of the Supply of Goods and Services Act 1982, which codified the existing law about services, contains a useful set of rules which all prudent traders will follow. First, section 13 says that where the supplier of a service is acting in the course of a business:

- there is an implied term that the supplier will carry out the service with reasonable care and skill.

This means that you will be presumed to know what you are doing should you agree to lay a fitted carpet, or tile a roof or adjust the brakes on a car. The very fact that you hold yourself out as possessing a particular skill means that the public are entitled to expect you at least to have the standard of an average person claiming to have the same skills.

 WARNING: Do not offer to do things unless you really have the skill and are properly trained or experienced.

Time in service contracts

As we have seen in Chapter 3 (page 45), in sale of goods contracts, where nothing is agreed, the seller has to come up with the goods within a 'reasonable' time.

Research into customer expectations of the way services are provided showed many complaints about delay. Although the 1982 Act does not lay down a time-table, it does summarise the law by saying in section 15:

- Where (in a service contract) … the time for the service to be carried out is not fixed by the contract, left to be fixed in a manner agreed by the contract or determined by the course of dealing between the parties, there is an implied term that the supplier will carry out the service within a reasonable time.

Each case depends on its own facts. In one reported case, a garage took eight weeks when a 'normally competent' repairer would have done the job in five; it was held that there had been unreasonable delay and compensation was awarded (*Charnock v. Liverpool Corporation (1968)*). If a reasonable time has elapsed, the customer can make time of the essence by serving notice.

Price in service contracts

Very similar rules apply about how much the customer has to pay in service contracts. Section 16 says:

- Where (in a service contract)...the consideration for the service is not fixed by the contract, left to be fixed in a manner agreed by the contract or determined by the course of dealing between the parties, there is an implied term that the (customer) will pay a reasonable price.

Bailment

There will be times when you are temporarily in possession of someone else's property. This is called 'bailment'. It covers a wide range of situations which the law divides into two classes.

First, 'gratuitous bailment' – where the owner leaves his property but does not pay anything. Examples would be:

- borrowing a neighbour's ladder
- leaving coats or bags in a cloakroom.

The 'bailee' – you – must treat it with the same sort of care as you would look after your own property.

Secondly, 'bailment for valuable consideration' – where charges are involved. This sort of bailment includes:

- warehousing
- paying to leave coats, bags etc
- garaging a car
- leaving jewellery for repair
- dry-cleaning, etc.

Here there are greater obligations on the bailee, depending on the type of property involved:

- you must take reasonable care of the item
- it must be kept in a suitable place
- it must be reasonably protected against danger.

So a jeweller must keep valuables in a safe and his shop must be reasonably burglar-proof. A cloakroom in a restaurant should not be open to the world. Apply common sense.

The most important thing to note is that you are not an 'insurer', liable for everything that happens. So if the jeweller has taken the steps outlined above, he would not be liable to the customer if the shop was burgled and valuables stolen.

Summary of Key Learning Points

1. Do __not__ put up notices which say 'no money back' or 'no refunds' or 'sale goods not taken back'.

2. Do __not__ have any contract term which says 'no warranty given' or 'sold as seen' or which tries to limit or avoid liability under the 1979 Act.

3. Remember that goods subject to 'title retention' do not belong to you; they cannot be used as security for credit, overdrafts, etc.

4. The right to lien is lost if you part with the goods; once they have left the shop you cannot take them back.

5. Don't confuse 'lien' with rights of ownership.

6. Make sure that you have adequate insurance to cover you should anything happen to goods before they are delivered to the consumer.

7. If you choose a carrier, you may be liable should anything go wrong.

8. If you arrange carriage for a customer, that contract will be a 'consumer' one even though you and the carrier are both commercial people. For legal purposes, you are the customer's agent.

9. In commercial contracts for the supply of services, limitation of these implied terms __is__ allowed, to the extent that the exclusion is 'fair and reasonable'.

10. Do not offer to do things unless you really have the skill and are properly trained or experienced.

Checklist

☞ Do we have trade or business customers? What must we do to avoid having unfair contracts terms and exclusion clauses?

☞ How much of our stock is subject to 'retention of title'? Does this affect our right to sell to customers? What happens if we get into financial difficulties?

☞ Are our contract terms unfair? What action should be take? Do we need any written terms at all?

☞ What are our systems for delivering goods to customers? Who is responsible if they are damaged or lost? Do we employ carriers? Are their terms reasonable? Do they meet the current law on 'small print'?

☞ When do we provide services to our customers? Are the relevant staff (or contractors) qualified or trained? Do the goods we supply in service contracts meet the test of 'satisfactory quality'?

☞ What training do we provide to ensure that staff have all the skills needed?

5

What Happens After a Contract

So far we have looked at the considerable legal duties imposed on retailers, and how many of them cannot be modified. Now it is time to see what obligations the customer has, because the contract between you is not one-sided.

There are three basic rules for customers set out in the Sale of Goods Act 1979. First, by section 27 customers must:

- pay for what they bought
- take delivery of the goods

and by section 37(1):

- not delay unreasonably in taking delivery.

Many customers believe that the basic law of contract somehow does not apply to them; they can make and break contracts at will without any fear of retribution. When they tell traders that they have 'changed their mind' they become very upset when it is pointed out that they have voluntarily entered into a legally binding arrangement. Just as you have to produce goods which conform to the contract, so they have to pay for them and take them away. The law says so.

What can you do if a person decides that he does not want the goods after all? From a practical point of view, it is really a question of goodwill. You may decide that it is better in the long run to agree to cancel the contract in the hope that the customer may come back and buy something else. If so, fine.

Payment

There are several ways in which a customer may pay what is due – cash, cheque, credit card, credit arrangement are the most common.

Cash

If you want to be pedantic, the customer is supposed to pay the exact amount in coin of the realm and there are rules about how many of each type of coin is 'legal tender'.

- Bronze coins (1p and 2p), up to 20p;
- Small 'silver' coins (5p and 10p), up to £5;
- Large 'silver' (20p and 50p), up to £10;
- £1, £2 or £5 coins – unlimited.

Bank of England notes are legal tender up to any amount in England and Wales (and are generally accepted in Scotland and Northern Ireland). Notes issued by banks in Scotland and Ulster are usually taken by traders in England and Wales (and certainly by banks) although they are not legal tender.

Most traders give change, although there is no legal requirement to do so and many machines carry notices stating that the exact money is required and no change given.

Cheques

Cheques are a perfectly good way for money to change hands, and, so long

as you follow the rules about cheque cards, you will be fully protected. Most of the problems that arise when traders are refused payment are because they have not been careful. Once the banks printed their requirements on the back of cheque cards; not so nowadays. However, in summary the rules are:

- the cheque must be in a chequebook
- the code number on the card must be the same as that on the customer's cheque
- the card must not have expired (the date is impressed on the card)
- the card must be signed
- the cheque must be signed in your presence
- the signature must correspond with that on the card
- you must write the cheque card number on the back of the cheque.

Follow these rules and the issuing bank will guarantee the payment of one cheque not exceeding the £50 (or higher) limit on the cheque card in any single transaction.

This is a very helpful system for traders. There is no need to ask for any other identification or the customer's address since the cheque will be met and you will be paid.

 WARNING: The rules protect one cheque not over the limit in any one transaction.

When the bill is over the limit, many traders ask for two (or more) cheques – one for £50 (or the limit), the other for the balance. They are at risk if the customer has insufficient money to meet the total bill. An attempt has been made to defeat the cheque card rules and the bank could refuse to honour both cheques.

Forged cheques

You may take some comfort from an Appeal Court case in 1993 (*First Sport Limited v Barclays Bank*) which concerned a forged cheque used with a cheque card. A crook went to a shop and bought some goods which he paid for with a cheque from a stolen chequebook backed with a stolen cheque guarantee card. All the rules set out in the bank's conditions were followed by the retailer and the signature on the cheque resembled that on

the card. The retailer therefore had no reason to doubt that the customer was the person who owned the chequebook.

The guarantee card had on the back a space for the customer's signature and bore the words 'the card may only be used by the authorised signatory'. This was the nub of the matter. When a crook signed a stolen cheque, how could he be the 'authorised signatory'? For the use of the cheque and the guarantee to be legally effective, the person proffering both had to have authority to convey the offer by the bank to the retailer (in order to make a contract with the bank).

The true owner of the card had such authority – but did a thief?

The court held that, provided the retailer had no reason to believe that the customer was *not* the authorised signatory and the account holder, the bearer of the cheque had ostensible authority to convey the bank's offer. When the retailer accepted by taking the cheque, the contract came into force and the bank was liable.

The bank argued that since 1882 the law had been that a cheque with a forged signature is not a cheque but a mere sham piece of paper with writing on it, and the bank on which it purports to be drawn has no liability. Nor may the bank debit the customer's account with the amount of the cheque.

However, two of the three judges concluded that the bank which issued the cheque and the card, by making a set of conditions to accompany a cheque card which the retailer followed to the letter, had made itself liable to meet the cheque when presented in good faith by the trader. They added that the bank could have worded the terms and conditions to the effect that a thief had no authority.

How on earth would a retailer have known whether or not the person in front of him had authority? The one thing that crooks rarely carry is anything enabling their true identity to be discovered. You can imagine their reply if you asked 'Did you steal this cheque book?'! Having photographs on cheque cards might be one way of trying to cope with this sort of fraud. One clearing bank is experimenting with this.

Stopping cheques

Sometimes a customer with a grievance will put a stop on a cheque. This can be an expensive mistake – for him. Stopping a cheque 'dishonours' it and may be extremely difficult for him to justify – unless what you sold

him has completely broken down and you refuse to offer a refund or a substitute. You are entitled to 'sue on the cheque' – that is, issue a summons for the amount of money written on the front of the cheque rather than suing the customer for breach of contract. This has advantages because the claim is a 'default' one where you should be able to obtain judgment much more quickly than in an 'ordinary' action.

Credit cards and credit generally are covered in the next chapter.

Estimates and quotations

Customers often complain that the final price they are charged for goods – and more often services – is different from the original quote. Whether they have any legally based complaint depends on how the original price was given.

An 'estimate' is what it sounds like: a reasonably accurate guess at the price for a completed job taking everything – measurements, labour costs, materials etc – into account. The final figure may be more or less; a margin of 15 per cent either way is probably acceptable. Within those limits the customer must pay.

A 'quotation' on the other hand is the price. That is what has to be paid; it is the limit that the trader can charge. If he makes a mistake in his sums, he has to stand the loss.

 WARNING: Make sure that any document is described either as 'estimate' or 'quotation' and that any terms and conditions do not contain both words (as often happens).

Value added tax

Any indication of the price of goods must state whether or not VAT is included (regulation 9, Price Marking Order 1999). There is no similar statutory rule for the price of services, though paragraph 2.2.6 of the Price Marking Code of Practice 1988 (see page 128) says:

● All price indications you give to private consumers, by whatever means, should include VAT.

Deposits and other down-payments

Deposits are a perennial source of anxiety as there are three different

situations where money paid in advance by a customer is called a 'deposit', but there is only one actual deposit.

Option

First, a customer goes to your shop, sees something he likes and asks whether it can be put on one side until the weekend so that he may come back with his wife and have another look. You say 'yes' but ask him to pay some money 'as a deposit'.

This payment is not a deposit. It amounts to the payment for an option for the customer to go back at the later date and decide whether or not to buy the item. If he does go ahead, you will almost always take the advance payment into account when fixing the price.

If the customer does not return by the time limit, he loses his money, as he also would if he does not come back because he decides not to buy. You have met your side of the option by holding the item and not selling it. Of course, if you failed to do this, you would have to give the customer his money back because you would then be in breach of your obligations under the option.

Part-payment of the price

The second situation is this. The customer makes a contract to buy goods at an agreed price. When the time comes to pay, he does not have enough cash on him. He offers to pay a proportion; you agree and put the goods away safely, marking the sales invoice: 'Price £x – deposit £y = balance due £x-y'.

Again, this is not a deposit. It is a part-payment of the purchase price. If the customer does not turn up and pay the remainder, you are not automatically allowed to forfeit the 'deposit' and re-sell the goods – because they are not yours. You may sue for the balance or treat the contract as repudiated and claim damages for breach of contract. These will generally be the loss of your profit on the sale, which may or may not be equivalent to the 'deposit' you are holding.

A true deposit

The only case where a true legal deposit arises is where you – as a condition of making the contract – insist that the customer makes a payment of money before the contract is made.

The test is simple. Will you agree to make a contract if the customer

does not pay the advance money? If the answer is no, the money paid will be a deposit. If the customer defaults, the deposit may be forfeited so long as it represents a pre-assessment of your likely loss and is not a 'penalty' for breaking the contract.

 WARNING: Spell out in simple terms why the customer is making the pre-payment.

When the customer breaks his contract

Your customer may return to say that he has changed his mind and he wants to get out of the contract. You have two ways of dealing with this situation which have different consequences:

- You may go along with the customer, let him off the contract – but claim from him the profit you lost; or
- You can refuse to accept his cancellation, hold him to the contract and sue for the price.

Later, we shall examine how disputes can be resolved (see Chapter 12).

There is another curiosity. The customer, having bought and paid for the goods, may simply not come and collect them.

 WARNING: You cannot sell something which does not belong to you.

What do you do? We saw in Chapter 2 that there were rules fixing the time for property to pass in the absence of any agreement. Well, you can have a simple term in your contract with customers which says:

- Property does not pass to the buyer until he takes delivery and removes the goods.

This would enable you to sell the goods if the customer never came back; the money would have to be held for him, of course. But you would be legally entitled to sell because you were still the true owner.

As normally risk passes with the change of ownership, you might need to modify this term to ensure that you remain owner but the risk of loss, damage etc falls on the buyer:

- The goods are at the risk of the buyer from the time of the contract;

but property does not pass to the buyer until he takes delivery and removes the goods.

The customer's failure to take delivery of the goods is a breach of the Sale of Goods Act 1979. Section 37 says:

- When the seller is ready and willing to deliver the goods, and requests the buyer to take delivery, and the buyer does not within a reasonable time...take delivery, he is liable to the seller for any loss (arising) from the refusal to take delivery and also for a reasonable charge for the care and custody of the goods.

This limits your claim to the cost of storage, etc. However, it may well be that the persistent failure to take delivery can be treated as 'repudiation' of the contract by the customer, in which case your remedy is to take the goods back, resell them and claim any loss from the customer.

Goods sold but not paid for

Here you are an 'unpaid seller' and the Sale of Goods Act 1979 gives you:

- a right of lien (see Chapter 4, page 68)
- a right to retain the goods
- a right to re-sell the goods.

Should the customer who bought the goods but did not pay for them never turn up, you can sell. Any shortfall can be claimed against the defaulting customer.

 WARNING: You must not harass a person who owes you money. You would be prosecuted (see page 202).

Working through the contract

Let us assume that the contract was properly made, the goods were delivered on time and the customer took them and paid all the money due to you.

Your problems are not necessarily over. Once he gets the goods home, the customer has the right to examine them and then to see if they do what he expects them to. Eventually, after some time has gone by, the customer will be said to have 'accepted' the goods; after that his legal rights are reduced.

Examination

Many things one buys these days come in boxes or packages; there is no way you can see whether they will work unless and until they are unpacked and – in the case of many household purchases – the product is plugged in or it is plumbed in. It would be quite unreasonable to tell someone that once the goods were in his house they would be assumed to be in perfect condition.

It is only natural that the customer should have the chance to check that everything is in order. This commonsense approach is reflected in section 34 of the Sale of Goods Act 1979:

- Unless otherwise agreed, when the seller tenders delivery of goods to the buyer, he is bound on request to afford the buyer a reasonable opportunity of examining the goods (to see) whether they are in conformity with the contract.

The first three words allow 'contracting out' but, as will be seen below, not in the case of sales to consumers. It is still possible for your suppliers to insert terms in their contacts which require you to notify any problem within a very short time. Such terms may well fall foul of the Unfair Contract Terms Act 1977.It may be unreasonable to expect you to open every package from a container load delivery in three days (or even seven days). To shut out any claim for redress for defective goods after that short time has passed is tantamount to the supplier avoiding liability for his own breach of contract and so is contrary to section 3 of the 1977 Act.

 WARNING: Read your suppliers' small print to see if there are time limits for notifying shortages, defects, etc.

Acceptance

This is one of the most critical parts of the whole deal between you and your customers. 'Acceptance' here does not mean the actual handing over of goods and is unrelated to the everyday use of the word. It is a legal word with a very serious legal meaning, for once a buyer of goods has 'accepted' them he loses forever the right to reject them, cancel the contract and claim his money back. He still has useful legal rights (as we shall see) but from his point of view the most important and certainly most

valuable one of calling the whole deal off is lost forever.

This part of the law was extensively revised by the Supply of Goods and Services Act 1994 which made important amendments to section 35 of the Sale of Goods Act 1979. Section 35(1) says that a buyer is 'deemed' to have accepted the goods:

- when he intimates to the seller that he has done so.

 WARNING: As between you and your supplier, there may be a term in the contract which contains words like 'the signature of the buyer shall be treated as acceptance for the purpose of the Sale of Goods Act 1979'.

However, the new law makes it almost impossible for an ordinary consumer to trap himself into acceptance (see below).

- when the goods have been delivered to him and he does any act in relation to them which is inconsistent with the ownership of the seller.

To understand this, one has to bear in mind that until the sale was completed the goods belonged to you – the seller. If the customer starts to use the goods – to wash clothes in a washing machine, or drive about in a car or wear a pair of shoes – the more he uses them the more difficult it is for him to say that he is still seeing if they conform to the contract and that they are, in effect, still your goods which he will return to you if he finds fault. There is also a considerable problem if what has been bought is fitted to something else – like a spare part for some machine – or is changed irreversibly as happens when bricks are turned into a house or timber is cut up and laid as joists.

I said earlier that a chance to examine is common sense. This is set out in section 35(2) of the 1979 Act:

- Where goods are delivered to the buyer, and he has not previously examined them, he is not deemed to have accepted them … until he has had a reasonable opportunity of examining them (to see) whether they are in conformity with the contract.

This stresses that examination is a *right* and that if any attempt is made to frustrate that right, the goods will not be treated as 'accepted' and the buyer retains the right to reject them and cancel the contract.

Of course one can argue just how far 'examination' should be taken; the Act does not have any definition, so the court would take a sensible approach. Certainly anyone buying something mechanical, electrical or electronic must be given a chance to see if it performs most of the principal functions.

Bearing in mind the list of ingredients in the new definition of 'satisfactory quality', there are now many other aspects of performance which the customer will be allowed to examine – appearance, freedom from minor defects, safety, etc. The new concept of 'durability' may make the judicial approach to 'acceptance' more difficult than anticipated.

Under the old law, a court held that it was reasonable for the buyer of a second-hand car to wait four months from the date of purchase before having serious defects investigated because (the judge said) 'until that date the buyer had not had any reasonable opportunity of ascertaining whether the vehicle conformed with the contract' (*M & T Consultants Ltd v. Grange Motors Ltd (1981)*). An extreme case perhaps, but one example of the way the courts may look at these problems.

Contrast it with another case where the court held that a motorist whose car seized up after only 120-odd miles and three weeks' use, had accepted the vehicle and was not entitled to his money back (Bernstein v Pamson Motors (1986)). That case was widely believed by lawyers to have been wrongly decided but before an appeal could be heard the parties came to terms.

Delivery notes

One of the vices which the Law Commission looked at when considering 'acceptance' was the widespread use of delivery notes, receipts, acceptance notes – any sort of document that consumers were asked to sign which contained small print stating that signature confirmed that the goods were received in good condition.

When he unpacked the goods and found a defect or fault, the consumer was told that he had signed a paper to say that the goods were all right and discovered that he had inadvertently given up his rights under the law. Although it was arguable that for anything delivered in packaging and left unopened the words 'good condition' could only refer to the container and not the goods themselves, this was never tested in court.

The new version of the Sale of Goods Act 1979 has made it clear that

this sort of approach to delivery notes is no longer satisfactory. Section 35(3) sets out a new inalienable right for consumers:

- ...the (consumer) buyer cannot lose his right to rely on subsection (2) (the right to examination) by agreement, waiver or otherwise.

 WARNING: Do not ask customers to sign delivery notes saying 'received in good condition'; treat it simply as a receipt proving delivery to the right person.

Acceptance by default

In most cases the ordinary buyer does not sign anything, nor is he refused a chance to make a proper examination. When does he 'accept' the goods?

Section 35(4) of the Sale of Goods Act 1979 deals with this commonest situation:

- The buyer...is deemed to have accepted the goods when after the lapse of a reasonable time he retains the goods without intimating to the seller that he has rejected them.

Here again is that wretched word 'reasonable' and the Act is no help in defining how long the 'reasonable time' might be. One can only look at the cases – all dealing with cars.

- *Bernstein v Pamsons (1986)* – a new car seized up after three weeks – buyer held to have accepted.
- *M & T Consultants Ltd v. Grange Motors Ltd (1981)* – second-hand car, buyer waited four months – held not to have accepted.
- *Lee v York Coach & Marine (1977)* – second-hand car broke down first day; buyer did not reject for six months – held that she must have accepted.

Obviously much depends on what was sold. Fresh food has a short life and so the buyer has a very short time in which to reject; a washing machine might not have all its programmes tested for several weeks. A camera bought in July for a gift next Christmas may not be taken from its box for many months.

Acts of ownership – do they hinder the customer?

Most people buy goods because they want them for some reason. What they principally expect is that their purchase will work and fulfil the need for which it was bought. They do not expect to find defects or to anticipate rejecting the goods.

When something goes wrong, therefore, their first reaction may well be to try to put right whatever is broken or not working properly. In many cases, too, a simple repair or adjustment will transform a useless product into one that works perfectly well.

In the past taking this reasonable step had two shortcomings. First it was treated as 'an act inconsistent with the ownership of the seller' and so would mean that the unfortunate buyer found that he had lost his right to reject. Secondly, leaving the defective item for repair meant that the 'reasonable time' was still running. So when, after some weeks (or months), it came back apparently repaired but still not working properly, he was told that he had 'accepted' because so much time had gone by.

Section 35(6)(a) of the Sale of Goods Act 1979 now makes it clear that attempts at curing a problem with defective goods do not of themselves amount to 'acceptance':

- The buyer is not...deemed to have accepted the goods merely because he asks for, or agrees to, their repair by or under an arrangement with the seller...

 WARNING: Having defective goods repaired stops the clock running for 'acceptance'.

The Act makes no reference to manufacturers' guarantees or warranties – which retailers often ask customers to use. I think that the words 'agrees to a repair under an arrangement with the seller' could mean invoking a guarantee because one would not have the benefit of any guarantee unless the goods had been sold by the retailer.

It was believed that if one bought goods and then sold them or gave them away acceptance had automatically taken place, thus preventing a retailer from making any claim back against his supplier. Section 35(6)(b) corrects that by adding that acceptance is not deemed because:

● the goods are delivered to another under a sub-sale or other disposition.

 WARNING: If your supply contract says that the right to reject is lost by any retail sale, the new Act cancels that term.

'Commercial units'

There are some cases where what is sold forms a recognisable unit – a pair of shoes or a set of encyclopedias, for example. It was felt that it would be unreasonable for a buyer to be able to keep one shoe or one volume from the set and reject the rest. Equally, it would not be right for a person to remove working parts from a dud car and reject the rest of the vehicle. To put this into legal form, a new part was added to section 35(7) of the Sale of Goods Act 1979:

● Where the contract is for the sale of goods making one or more commercial units, a buyer accepting any goods included in a unit is deemed to have accepted all the goods making the unit.

'Commercial unit' is defined as a unit of which division would materially impair the value of the goods or the character of the unit.

No one knows whether this would apply to a suite of furniture.

Partial rejection

The customary rule of law was that a person who accepted some of the contract goods was treated as having accepted them all. He could not reject the defective ones and keep the rest; he had to choose to keep all or reject all.

Now, unless the parties agree otherwise, the buyer is given a general right of partial rejection where some of the goods do not conform to the contract, for whatever reason. Section 35A(1) of the Sale of Goods Act 1979 improves the consumer buyer's situation by saying:

● If the buyer-
(a) has a right to reject the goods by reason of a breach on the part of the seller that affects some or all of them, but
(b) accepts some of the goods, including, where there are any goods unaffected by the breach, all such goods, he does not by accepting them lose his right to reject the rest.

The consequence of this is as follows. The buyer may:

- accept all the conforming goods and reject the rest which do not conform
- accept all the conforming goods and some which do not, rejecting the rest
- reject all the goods
- keep all the goods
- keep most of the goods but reject only the most defective.

This new right is a particular help to consumers who buy DIY materials, especially when they have to buy something which comes in a carton containing a certain number. For example, if you bought 100 tiles and found, on delivery, that 40 were cracked you can now retain the 60 good ones and reject the 40; or retain the 60 and some of the duff 40 (to use parts of by cutting) and reject the rest; but the right to reject them all is not lost.

Note: If you do not want your customers to have this right, you are perfectly entitled to have a contract term which excludes the impact of section 35A – for example:

- The buyer is not entitled to any right of partial rejection of any goods comprised in this contract.

Rejection

To appreciate the legal significance of all that has been said about 'acceptance', you need to understand the buyer's rights.

If goods are delivered, etc., and he examines them and then at some early stage discovers a fault, there is a breach of contract. This amounts to a breach of one or more of the implied terms in section 13 and 14 of the Sale of Goods Act. If the defect is fundamental – the goods are not as they were described or will not do what they are supposed to do, or are damaged or have a poor finish (any of the 'ingredients' of satisfactory quality are lacking) – the breach of contract is a 'breach of condition'.

Under the general law of contract, the remedy for a 'breach of condition' is a right to cancel the contract, return the goods to the seller and reclaim the price plus any other out-of-pocket expense.

It is essential that any aggrieved buyer – whether a consumer or a trader – who wishes to take advantage of this important legal remedy makes a formal 'rejection' of the defective goods. In many cases, complaints are

sorted out without difficulty over the counter by word of mouth. But where there is a dispute about whether there is a defect or a claim that the fault was caused by something that the buyer did, it can be critical for the buyer to put his intention in writing using the word 'rejection'.

- The (goods) you sold me on (date) do not work; there is an inherent fault amounting to a breach of the implied terms in section 13/14/15 of the Sale of Goods Act 1979 (as amended).

 I hereby reject the goods which now stand at your risk ready for your collection. I shall be grateful if you will send me a refund of the price of £x and £y to cover the out-of-pocket expenses (describe) caused by the goods not doing what they were supposed to.

In *Lee v York Coach & Marine (1977)*, Mrs Lee knew on the very first day she bought her used car that it was badly defective. She contacted the garage and weeks of argument took place. But it was not until she started court action six months later that the word 'reject' was first used – and the judge held that it was too late.

Returning rejected goods

There is no legal requirement for a buyer to bring faulty goods back to the shop where he bought them, unless there is a term in the contract which says that he must. Your contract with your customer might read:

- All defective goods must be returned to the seller's premises in the event of any claim for breach of contract.

As we shall see (page 210), if he established his claim, the disgruntled buyer is entitled to his money back and other expenses, which might include the cost of taking the goods back to your shop. You may care to weigh the advantages of making him bring things back to you.

New remedies for consumers

From 31 March 2003, a new Part 5A is added to Sale of Goods Act 1979 by the Sale and Supply of Goods to Consumers Regulations 2002.

Where a consumer buys goods which do not 'conform' to the contract (which means there has been a breach of an implied term – see above), section 48A provides that the consumer will have the right to one of the

following: a repair or replacement; a reduction in the price; rescission.

A vital new presumption is found in s.48A(3) which says that goods which do not conform within six months of delivery, must be taken not to have conformed at that date. I will deal with that below.

Section 48B deals with the first two. The buyer can demand a repair, or a replacement within a reasonable time, unless such a remedy is impossible, or is disproportionate in comparison to other remedies or to a reduction in the price.

A remedy is disproportionate if it imposes unreasonable costs on the seller taking into account the value of the goods had they conformed, the significance of the lack of conformity and whether another remedy is (in effect) simpler and more appropriate.

Section 48C provides that a reduction in price or rescission may be demanded by the consumer if the goods can neither be repaired nor replaced, or if one of those remedies has been sought but the seller does not provide it within a reasonable time. Upon any rescission, the repayment to the buyer may be reduced to take account of the use he has had since delivery – an interesting development.

The new law recognises that many consumers actually want a replacement for a defective item. Retailers have often refused this on the ground that they may be prejudicing themselves. Non-lawyers are also uncertain about the legal status of a replacement. These new remedies available to a consumer are therefore to be welcomed, particularly the option of a repair. To insist on replacement of an item with what appears to be a major defect but which can be made perfect by a simple or inexpensive repair is wholly unreasonable.

Throughout the lengthy consultation process, one point was made repeatedly – that there must be a correlation between the new remedies and 'acceptance' as set out in section 35 (see above in this chapter). The regulations deal with this up to a point. Section 48A(3) says (in paraphrase) that any defect which is discovered within six months is deemed to have existed at the time of delivery. Section 48D says that if the buyer invokes the right to repair or replacement, he cannot reject the goods and terminate the contract for breach of condition until the seller has had a reasonable time in which to repair/replace etc.

There is a belief that the combined effect of these two provisions is giving status to a general principle that the famous 'reasonable time' within s.35(4) of the Sale of Goods Act is up to six months. This may

remove some of the uncertainties which have existed for some time.

Section 48E gives powers to the court to make orders for specific performance or to proceed as if the buyer had required repair, replacement, reduction or rescission.

Similar amendments are made to the Supply of Goods and Services Act 1982 relating to goods which are supplied to a consumer in the course of a contract for the services.

The Supply of Goods (Implied Terms) Act 1973 – which inserted implied terms as to quality and fitness of goods supplied under hire-purchase agreements – is also amended but only to take account of the 'public statements' provision described above. So people who buy goods in this way will have less protection than ordinary consumers who pay cash or use other forms of credit.

Summary

The regulations really offer consumers an alternative. They can use existing law, reject defective goods as soon as they become aware of the trouble and demand their money back, relying on a tried and tested legal method. They have to be aware of the problems of 'acceptance' within section 35. Or they can choose to use the new regime and look for repair, replacement, reduction in price or rescission. To what extent this will catch on, rather than muddle people on both sides of the counter, remains to be seen.

Guidance notes are available from the Regulatory Guidance page of the Department of Trade and Industry website: dti.gov.uk

 WARNING: A consumer is legally entitled to claim a repair or replacement if goods fail within six months.

 WARNING: If you do not repair the goods, or have no replacement, a consumer is legally entitled to a reduction in the price or a refund.

Summary of Key Learning Points

1. The rules protect <u>one</u> cheque not over the limit in <u>any one transaction</u>.

2. Make sure that any document is described either as 'estimate' or 'quotation' – and that any terms and conditions do not contain both words (as often happens).

3. Spell out in simple terms why the customer is making the pre-payment.

4. You cannot sell something which does not belong to you.

5. You must <u>not</u> harass a person who owes you money. You could be prosecuted.

6. Read your suppliers' small print to see if there are time limits for notifying shortages, defects, etc.

7. As between you and your supplier, there may be a term in the contract which contains words like 'the signature of the buyer shall be treated as acceptance for the purpose of the Sale of Goods Act 1979'.

8. Do not ask customers to sign delivery notes saying 'received in good condition'; treat it simply as a receipt proving delivery to the right person.

9. Having defective goods repaired stops the clock running for 'acceptance'.

10. If your supply contract says that the right to reject is lost by any retail sale, the new Act cancels that term.

11. A consumer is legally entitled to claim a repair or replacement if goods fail within six months.

12. If you do not repair the goods, or have no replacement, a consumer is legally entitled to a reduction in the price or a refund.

Checklist

 What system do we have about payment for what we sell:

- for cash?
- by cheque?

Do these meet the banks' rules? Do sales staff follow them to the letter?

 What do our estimates and quotation documents say? Do we explain the difference between the two? Are the staff trained not to confuse them?

 Are our pricing policies legal?

 How do we handle:

- deposits?
- part-payments?
- customers who change their minds?
- customers who do not pay on time?

 When we receive deliveries, what are our systems for:

- checking and inspecting?
- notifying shortages/breakages/damage?
- checking goods against delivery notes?
- authorising signature of acceptance notes?

 Who is responsible for making a firm decision about deliveries? How quickly are problems about delivery solved? How do we cope with customers demanding their goods?

 What records do you keep of the date when goods are sold?

 Are staff trained to respond correctly when customers ask for a repair or refund?

6

You and Credit

There are very few traders who do not offer credit facilities of one kind or another. Since the late 1970s there has been considerable regulation of providers of credit, advertising and documents. The main legislation is the Consumer Credit Act 1974 and the huge range of regulations made under the Act which is administered centrally by the Director General of Fair Trading, and enforced locally by Trading Standards Departments.

Licensing

By section 21 of the Consumer Credit Act 1974, everyone – a limited company, partnership or a sole trader – who lends his own money to customers must have a '*consumer credit licence*'. The only exceptions are where:

- the lending is only to limited companies
- credit is always over the upper limit in the Act (at present £15,000).

In addition, although there is only one type of *licence*, there are a number of different *categories* depending on what you do, for which a licence is required. For example, everyone who introduces customers to sources of credit (that is, does not lend his own money but enables customers to take out hire-purchase and other types of credit) must have a licence which includes a '*credit-broking*' category. If you carry out more than one type of credit business, your licence must incorporate all appropriate categories of licensable activity.

Canvassing credit

Section 23(3) of the Consumer Credit Act 1974 imposes restrictions on the canvassing of credit. The only circumstances where a person can be authorised to canvass credit away from trade premises are those where the seller provides the goods but not the finance itself (what are called '*debtor-creditor-supplier*' transactions).

It is not possible to authorise a person to canvass the direct provision of credit on the doorstep by 'cold calling'. Special provisions apply to moneylenders etc; they must have received a prior written request from the customer. Breaching this requirement risks criminal proceedings.

Who is entitled to a licence?

Anyone may apply to the Director General for a licence but the intention underlying the Act is that unsuitable people should be identified and eliminated. There are many things to be investigated, starting with the name under which the applicant is intending to carry on business. It must not be misleading or undesirable. The applicant must be a 'fit person' and section 25 of the Act sets out a long list of points to be considered.

The Director General will have regard to all the relevant circumstances and any evidence tending to show that the applicant (*or any of his employees, agents or associates, whether past or present*) has:

- committed any offence involving fraud, other dishonesty or violence
- contravened any provision under the Consumer Credit Act, or any other Act regulating credit
- discriminated on grounds of sex, colour, race or ethnic origins, or in connection with any business
- engaged in business practices appearing to the Director General to be deceitful or oppressive or otherwise unfair or improper (whether unlawful or not).

This gives enormous scope to weed out people who may have no convictions but whose methods are suspect. It also means that any prospective applicant must vet his staff and colleagues with great care because of the power of the Director General to refuse a licence on the grounds of the unsuitability of your employees. There is an appeal system if you believe the refusal of a licence was unfair.

Even if a licence is granted, the Act gives the Director General power to suspend or revoke it. This can be done if he later discovers some skeleton which was not apparent at the time of the original application or if later behaviour makes you unfit.

 WARNING: Just because you hold a credit licence does not give you the right to act in an unsuitable way. It can be taken away.

Changes

You will have to apply to the Director General to vary any licence if any of the following events take place:

- the name of the licensee is changed
- the name of any licensed business is changed
- another category of business is added
- canvassing off trade premises is planned.

Licence fees and duration

You will have to pay fees for all licences, authorisations and variations. A standard licence lasts for fifteen years; thereafter it has to be renewed. Current fees for new licences and for renewals are:

- Sole trader £70
- Partnership or company £175
- Variation £15
- Adding canvassing to existing licence £15

The Office of Fair Trading produces a wide range of extremely helpful material, including guidance about the need for licences. Information is available from:

> Office of Fair Trading
> Consumer Credit Licensing Branch
> Craven House
> 40 Uxbridge Road
> Ealing
> London W5 2BS
> Telephone: 0171-269 8608

or from your local Trading Standards Department.

Why bother with a licence?

Many traders regard regulation as petty bureaucracy and try to ignore it. If you are involved in any way with credit, there are two reasons why you must comply. Failure to hold a licence means that:

● you commit a criminal offence.

You have seen that any applicant has to be a 'fit person' and needs to have a clean record. Being convicted of trading without a licence would put at risk any chance of obtaining a licence.

Failure to hold a licence also means that:

● your agreements are unenforceable.

In economic terms this may be more important because, in order to sue anyone or take any action under a credit agreement, you would have to ask the Director General to allow you to proceed. He will make an order under section 40(2) of the Consumer Credit Act 1974 (which is familiarly known as a 'validation order') only if you can convince him that your failure to obtain a licence was due to a mistake rather than a deliberate flouting of the law – and that the customer was not at any disadvantage.

Section 40(3) of the Act says that the Director General shall consider all relevant factors including:

● whether the customers were prejudiced
● whether he would have granted a licence if you had applied properly
● how blameworthy was your failure to apply for a licence.

You will have to supply:

● full details of each agreement – date, parties, amount of credit, etc.
● details of any court action pending
● information about how you discovered that you were unlicensed and what you did to rectify the situation.

The fees payable are based on the number of unlicensed transactions:

● For the first 20 transactions £500
● For the first 100 transactions £1,000
● For each further 100 or part of 100 transactions £250
 (maximum £20,000)

For example, if you discovered that you had no licence and 1,373 agreements had been made, the fee in support of your application for a validation order would be:

For first 100	£1,000
next 1200 = 12 x £250	£3,000
next 73 = 1 x £250	£ 250
	£4.250

WARNING: If you are an unlicensed credit-broker, the agreements made by the main creditor cannot be enforced unless he applies for a validation order.

Other activities needing a licence

The Consumer Credit Act 1974 controls not only credit and credit-broking and hire; it extends to what the Act calls 'ancillary credit businesses':

- credit reference agencies
- debt-collecting
- debt-adjusting
- debt-counselling.

WARNING: When you run credit checks, make sure the company is respectable and licensed.

Plastic cards

The Consumer Credit Act 1974 does not refer anywhere to credit cards but, because it foresaw developments which might make a definition restrictive, talks of 'credit tokens', which it defines (in section 14) as:

- … a card, check, voucher, coupon, stamp, form, booklet or other document or thing given to an individual …

enabling him, by producing the token, to obtain cash, goods or services on credit – either from the issuer of the token or via an intermediary.

There are many types of plastic cards which you will see in your shop:

- credit cards
- cheque guarantee cards
- debit cards

- charge cards
- cash cards.

To add to the complications some have several functions.

Because of an outcry in the early 1970s when some British banks sent credit cards to virtually all existing customers, the Act bans the mass-mailing of credit tokens in remarkably unambiguous language in section 51:

- It is an offence to give a person a credit token if he has not asked for it.

 WARNING: The only way you can try to attract a customer to have a card is to let him have an application form plus all the terms and conditions; then it is up to him.

 WARNING: Do otherwise and you commit a criminal offence.

Credit cards

These may be issued by banks, building societies and other financial

bodies. They work this way. The customer goes to a trader (who is usually called, for these purposes, a 'merchant') and buys goods or services. The merchant takes the card, gives the customer a voucher (unless the arrangement is by post or phone) which he signs and which authorises the transaction.

The merchant then presents the voucher to the card issuer, who pays him the amount due from the customer – less a percentage.

In due course, the card issuer sends a statement to the customer, who pays either the full amount of the balance or a proportion, leaving the rest to attract interest and be paid off by instalments.

Credit cards also allow the customer to obtain cash.

Although there are all sorts of card issuers, the mechanics of processing is carried out by Visa or Mastercard, whose symbols will appear on the credit cards.

Cheque guarantee cards

The use of these cards has already been considered (see page 80). Legally, if they merely guarantee the payment of a given sum on a cheque, they are not credit tokens.

Debit cards

This sort of card is becoming more common. The customer uses it to obtain goods or services from a trader who, by being handed the card, is authorised to take the money from the customer's account – either directly at his bank, etc., or through an intermediary who provides processing services.

Credit advertising

The present regime for controlling the advertising of credit is contained in the Consumer Credit (Advertising) Regulations 1989.

There are three types of credit advertisement: 'simple', 'intermediate' and 'full'; what has to be said in each varies according to the type. The Office of Fair Trading produces excellent free booklets and information.

Simple credit advertisement
(Regulation 2 and Schedule 1 Part I)

- Maximum optional information permitted:
 - name of advertiser
 - his logo and/or trade association logo
 - postal address
 - telephone number
 - other information except indication of willingness to provide credit, or cash or any other price of goods, etc.

Intermediate credit advertisement
(Regulation 2 and Schedule 1 Part II)

- Compulsory information:
 - name of advertiser, postal address and/or phone number
 except (a) adverts at premises of dealer/creditor which customers not intended to take away
 (b) adverts with dealer's name and address
 (c) adverts with name/address/phone number of credit-broker
 - home mortgage warning (if appropriate)
 - insurance required (if appropriate)
 - deposit required (if appropriate)
 - credit-brokers' fee (if appropriate)
 - written information/quotation on request
 - foreign currency mortgage warning (if appropriate)
 - cash price (if appropriate)
 - APR (if appropriate) must be given where cash price is shown
 - APR may be variable
 - optional information (see below).

- Optional information in an intermediate credit advert:
 - his logo and/or trade association logo
 - occupation
 - credit facilities available and period
 - details of restricted classes
 - APR (if not shown above)
 - if APR given – interest rate
 - amount of credit or max/min credit

- security not affecting home
- if APR given – amount of advance payment
- different treatment of cash/credit customers
- name and address or phone no of creditor.

Full credit advertisement
(Regulation 2 and Schedule 1 Part III)

- Compulsory information:
 - name of advertiser, postal address;
 - except (a) adverts at premises of dealer/ creditor which customers not intended to take away
 - (b) adverts with dealer's name and address
 - (c) adverts with name/address/phone number of credit-broker
 - home mortgage warning (if appropriate)
 - insurance required (if appropriate)
 - deposit required (if appropriate)
 - details of other security apart from home
 - credit-broker's fee (if appropriate)
 - written information/quotation on request
 - foreign currency mortgage warning (if appropriate)
 - details of restricted classes and/or treatment of customers
 - frequency, number and amount of advance payments
 - cash price
 - APR; must be given:
 - (a) where cash price is shown
 - (b) where interest rate given
 - (c) where advert shows advance payment required
 - APR may be variable
 - frequency, number and amount of credit repayments
 - total amount payable by debtor
 - other payments and charges payable by debtor.

Schedule 3 allows for the use of representative information in the calculation of the total charge for credit and the APR.

- General rules: (Regulation 7)
 - a credit advert must NOT include:
 - (a) any indication that the terms of a credit agreement

imposes lesser expense or obligation than imposed by others except in a 'full' advert which shows as clearly a proper comparison

(b) 'interest free' – unless total amount payable does not exceed cash price

(c) 'no deposit' – except where no advance payment is required.

- (Regulation 8)
 - the APR must be:
 (a) given GREATER prominence than any other rate of charge
 (b) no less prominent than reference to the: period; deposit (or 'no deposit'); amount/number/frequency of payments/ instalments.

- (Regulation 2)
 - All prescribed information shall be clear and easily legible and (apart from name and address or phone (number) shown as a whole).

- (Regulation 6) – 'in-store' intermediate or full adverts.
 - Part of prescribed information may be 'conspicuously displayed' in any part of trader's premises – for example, 'beds available on credit' -
 - *so long as* there is
 - *either*: *no* cash price
 - *or* cash price plus APR and other compulsory information
 - *and* on the goods themselves there is a ticket or label showing the cash price, and total amount payable.

In-store adverts

You may not realise that a price ticket on goods in your shop is an advertisement. So that you do not have to print a great deal of information on price labels, the Act allows basic information on a price ticket or barker card – so long as you make it clear that the main information is available in the shop. Provided this is done, your price ticket need only contain:

- the cash price

- a signpost that details are available in-store
- the APR.

Nearby there must be all the information which has to be set out in an intermediate advert.

What is the APR?

The whole basis of 'truth-in-lending' is that the public should have information supplied to them in a uniform way to enable them to make sensible comparisons about the cost of credit. This is supposedly achieved by requiring interest rates to be quoted – not as flat rates, which most people understand, but by calculating the 'real' cost of interest – the APR or 'Annual Percentage Rate of charge'.

So far so good; the trouble is that the APR will vary depending on the length of the credit agreement and the intervals between instalments. This means that paying the same amount of loan over three years by quarterly, monthly or weekly instalments gives three different APRs, though the total money handed over will be the same in each case. It does not follow that the lowest APR is necessarily the cheapest or the best for a customer; it can mean that he is paying smaller instalments for a longer period.

There are huge books of tables showing APRs – an industry exists in doing background work for lenders, traders and trade associations. Nonetheless, about three quarters of the population has no idea what APR means (though a substantial minority think it means April!).

What is the difference between the APR and flat rates of interest?

The simplest way to explain this is to give an example.

If you borrow £100 at 20% interest and agree to pay it back at the end of 12 months, you have £100 available to you throughout the whole period of the loan. On the last day you pay back £120. The flat rate is 20%; the APR is 20% too,

But if you borrow at 20% interest and repay £10 on the last day of each of the 12 months, although you have £100 available on the first day, by midway you only have about £50 in hand (because you have repaid about half the loan). So, on a yearly basis, the interest of 20% is chargeable, not on the actual sum borrowed, but on the value of the average amount of credit you have throughout the year – which is about £50. The interest you

have agreed to pay is £20, but that as a percentage of £50 is 40%. The flat rate is 20% but the APR to be quoted in any advert would be 40%.

Refunds for goods bought with credit cards

This is an area of considerable misunderstanding and irritation. A customer buys goods from you and pays by credit card. He takes them away and then finds a defect justifying their return; a refund is agreed and the customer expects cash. You say that as he paid by plastic, the refund will be made the same way.

You are legally correct. By agreeing to accept the customer's credit card as a means of payment, you and he implicitly agree to the various terms for the use of the card. His are set out in the agreement he made with the card-issuer; yours, as a 'merchant', with the card issuer.

At the time of payment no cash changed hands; therefore on a refund being due, no cash will change hands either. The best thing is to state this in the shop.

 WARNING: Make it clear that when goods or services are bought with credit cards, any refunds are made by a credit on the customer's credit card account and not by cash.

Debit cards and refunds

The same principle applies to the use of Switch and Delta cards, which allow money to be taken directly from a customer's bank account and transferred to yours. When the system has to go in reverse, on a refund being made, you are fully within your rights to use the same method to credit the customer.

Customers who use credit cards to buy airline or theatre tickets or other services by telephone, giving a credit card number, do not expect a refund to be made in any other way.

Joint and several liability

As you will have gathered from what we have said earlier, a person who buys goods (or services) which turn out to be defective has a legal claim against the retailer because of the contract between them.

Where the customer bought the goods, etc., through a credit agreement

made as a result of pre-existing arrangements (or in contemplation of future arrangements) between the seller and a financial institution, he has additional rights under section 75 of the Consumer Credit Act 1974. Examples of such arrangements include:

- a garage selling a car and putting the customer in touch with a lender for a personal loan (not hire-purchase)
- buying goods or services with a credit card
- using trading checks.

In these cases the customer has a claim against the retailer (of course, because he sold the goods) and/or against the creditor – for misrepresentation or breach of contract. He may make a claim against whoever is the more accessible.

This is a very useful remedy if the retailer is in financial difficulties or has gone into liquidation. The creditor has to meet the claim, but retains rights to recover against the defaulting trader.

The Act excludes non-commercial agreements and any claim under £100.

Discrimination in credit

You must be careful not to discriminate against women (or men) when dealing with credit applications. The Sex Discrimination Act 1975 outlaws two types of discrimination:

- direct discrimination, where you treat a woman differently from a man (or vice versa) – for example, asking for a guarantor from one but not the other
- indirect discrimination, where an applicant for credit cannot meet your test – for example, a condition saying that a person must be a 'householder' discriminates against women because the owner or tenant or person whose name is on the rent book tends to be male.

Here are some ideas to avoid this sort of unlawful treatment:

- take the tenancy of either husband or wife as applying to both
- treat ownership of a house by either spouse as belonging to each;
- do not look down on part-timers
- do not disregard people on short contracts
- make sure that point-score systems avoid words such as 'housewife', 'salesman', 'postman' which are themselves selective.

Hire purchase and credit sale

Under a hire-purchase agreement, the customer sees goods in your shop and indicates that he wants to have them. You then sell them to a creditor which in turn hires them to the customer. His legal relationship under the HP agreement is with the creditor and not you; if the goods are defective, he must make any claim against the creditor (under the Supply of Goods (Implied Terms) Act 1973).

The goods remain the property of the creditor until the customer has paid the last instalment, when they finally become his.

A credit-sale agreement is different. The customer buys the goods from you; they become his property and he has a claim against you (as seller) if there are any defects.

Offer and acceptance

The same principles apply to these contracts as to all others. One important matter to understand is that the completion of an application form for credit is not the same thing as making a contract. Legally, the form, completed and signed by the customer, amounts to an 'offer' to enter into an agreement. Then it is up to the creditor to make enquiries before deciding whether or not to 'accept' the offer.

The creditor usually does this by having the form (already signed by the customer) signed on their behalf. There is, therefore, no transfer of the goods unless and until a hire-purchase agreement actually comes into existence by being signed by the creditor.

This means that the customer can change his mind and give notice to withdraw from the proposed HP agreement at any time until it is accepted by the creditor. If the goods have been supplied to the customer, he must return them.

If the customer gives you notice to withdraw, that will be treated as notice to the creditor and bring the matter to an end.

Cooling-off

Sometimes credit agreements (of all sorts) are signed away from trade premises. The customer may take the form home to sign or the trader may call on the customer. In this case, the Consumer Credit Act 1974 says that:

- the agreement will be 'cancellable' by the customer.

The right to cancel works this way. The 'cooling-off' period runs from the date the customer receives the agreement to sign and ends at the end of the fifth day after the day on which he receives the second copy of the agreement from the creditor or you.

Look at it this way:

- Customer signs first copy 1 July
- Second copy reaches customer by post
 (the Act says 'within seven days') 7 July
- Cooling-off period 5 days 12 July

If the second copy arrives late, the time is even longer, because the five days do not start until the customer receives that copy.

Legal rights under a HP agreement

Remember that the goods do not belong to you or to the customer; they are the property of the creditor.

The customer must:

- maintain them in good order
- pay the instalments on time
- not sell them.

The creditor may repossess the goods if the customer stops paying the instalments and less than one third of the whole debt has been paid. Otherwise, a court order must be obtained.

The customer has the right to end an HP agreement:

- by returning the goods, and
- paying enough to make one half of the total price.

The creditor – or you, if you are financing the hire-purchase yourself – have the same sort of obligations as under the Sale of Goods Act. The goods must be:

- of satisfactory quality
- fit for their intended use
- corresponding to any description.

Credit sale

Here the legal situation is the same as under the Sale of Goods Act. In addition, the customer has to:

- pay the instalments on time
- repay the whole balance if the goods are sold.

He cannot end the agreement by returning the goods and paying half the debt.

Extortionate credit bargains

The Consumer Credit Act 1974 enables people who feel that they have been badly treated by creditors to ask the court to intervene. This right applies where the borrower is 'an individual', which means that it applies to sole traders or partners as well as customers. The Act says that:

- a credit bargain is extortionate if it
 - requires the debtor to make payments which are grossly exorbitant, or
 - otherwise contravenes ordinary principles of fair dealing.

The court is required to take into account:

- the age, experience, business capacity and state of health of the borrower
- the degree of financial pressure he was under
- the risk accepted by the lender, his relationship to the borrower, whether the price was higher to make the credit seem lower and interest rates generally.

The Act allows agreements to be reopened at any time – even after they have been paid off. Although this seems like a very useful piece of consumer protection there have only been a tiny number of cases and very few debtors have been successful.

Special rules about cars and hire purchase

The Hire Purchase Act 1964 tried to help consumers who bought motor vehicles and discovered later that they were the subject of hire-purchase agreements. Under the normal rule, the innocent purchaser could receive

no better title than the seller could pass, and as the seller of a car on HP had no title, neither had the buyer. The finance house was perfectly entitled to trace and recover the car. The innocent victim was left with the right to sue the person who sold him the car – who was often untraceable or had no assets.

Under section 27 of the Act protection is given in certain circumstances. To qualify, a vehicle must have been sold to a person ('the crook') on a hire-purchase agreement. Before the end of the HP agreement, the crook sells the vehicle.

- Sale by the crook to an innocent buyer without notice of the HP, or
- sale by the crook to a garage (or finance house) who then sell to an innocent buyer without notice of the HP -

passes good title to that buyer.

However, that is the extent of the benefit because:

- Sale by crook to innocent buyer with notice, or
- sale by crook to innocent buyer with notice who then sells to innocent buyer without notice –

passes no title to the latter innocent buyer.

- Vehicle on HP is stolen; thief sells to innocent buyer without notice of either HP or theft –

no title passes.

Summary of Key Learning Points

1. Just because you hold a credit licence does not give you the right to act in an unsuitable way. It can be taken away.

2. If you are an unlicensed credit-broker, the agreements made by the main creditor cannot be enforced unless he applies for a validation order.

3. When you run credit checks, make sure the company is respectable and licensed.

4. The only way you can try to attract a customer to have a card is to let him have an application form plus all the terms and conditions; then it is up to him.

5. Do otherwise and you commit a criminal offence.

6. Make it clear that when goods or services are bought with credit cards, any refunds are made by a credit on the customer's credit card account and not by cash.

 Checklist

☞ Do we need a consumer credit licence? Is our current licence valid?

☞ Are we involved in any other business that needs a credit licence such as:

- credit reference agency?
- debt collecting?
- debt adjusting or counselling?
- hiring goods?

☞ Do our credit advertisements comply with the statutory rules? How can we check that they do? Do our PR people know? Do we have legal guidance? If not, should we?

☞ Do our price tickets contain all the APR data? Are there full credit adverts nearby in each department?

☞ How do we deal with refunds? Do we tell our customers before they pay by credit card?

☞ Do our credit application systems avoid discrimination?

☞ How do we deal with 'cooling off' periods?

☞ Can all our senior staff deal with detailed questions:

- about credit generally?
- about particular types of credit?
- about our policy on credit?

7

Criminal Law: Retailing Generally

Most of what we have said so far has been concerned with the 'civil law' – that is, the rules which regulate the way you deal with your suppliers and your customers. Any problems are matters for the individuals involved to sort out; if all else fails they will be resolved in the county court (or the High Court, if the sum at stake is large).

However, there is a large body of law where the sanctions are not civil 'damages' but fines – or even imprisonment. The criminal law is intended to protect society as a whole and to punish those who are dishonest or who put others in danger or at risk.

Because it has always been recognised that traders selling basic foodstuffs could take advantage of their customers, there have been laws about weights and measures and trying to prevent food adulteration since time immemorial. In the last thirty years laws have been brought in to encourage honesty about the way things are described and how prices are marked. There has also been a revolution in the legal requirements about the safety of goods and how they are displayed.

Much of the criminal law is based on commonsense and sound practice; traders whose principles are based on such ideals will have little to fear. Enforcement officers will concentrate their efforts on the small band of people who either ignore consumer protection law or who believe that they can find ways around it.

 WARNING: Breaking the criminal law, however inadvertently, can have expensive consequences. Make sure you keep up to date with changes and have skilled legal advice on anything you do not understand.

Trade Descriptions Act 1968

This Act not only covers the situation where a trader's customers are private individuals – ordinary shoppers. It also applies to dealings between traders and commercial buyers, and between retailers and their suppliers.

However, the Act only applies to descriptions made 'in the course of a trade or business' – so ruling out any criminal liability for anyone advertising or talking about goods for private sale.

It is an offence under this Act for a trader to describe inaccurately the goods that he sells. It also controls false statements about services and facilities and accommodation.

False trade descriptions

Section 1 of the Trade Descriptions Act 1968 contains three separate offences:

- Section 1(1)(a) – to apply a false trade description to any goods
- Section 1(1)(b) – to supply, or offer to supply any goods to which a false trade description is applied.

The second offence means that any trader can be prosecuted for having goods to which someone else has applied a false trade description – a manufacturer in an advertisement or brochure; an importer who attached a label. And the goods do not have to be sold or any customer actually prejudiced for an offence to be committed. Simply having merchandise on your premises carrying the false description is enough for you to be prosecuted, since 'offer to supply' is deemed to include both exposing and possessing the goods.

 WARNING: If anyone complains that information is wrong, an advertisement is misleading or a label inaccurate, do not argue. Offer a refund.

How does one tell if a description is illegal?
Section 3 of the Trade Descriptions Act 1968 says that:

- a false trade description is one which is false to a material degree

and adds, in section 3(2) that:

- a trade description which, though not false, is misleading – that is

to say, likely to be taken for an indication of any of the matters (in the list above) as would be false to a material degree – shall be deemed to be a false trade description.

This looks rather complicated, but you should try to look at the situation in the light of the following questions:

1 Has a trade description been applied?
2 Was it a false trade description?
3 If so, was it false to a material degree?
4 If not false, would it mislead the average shopper?

Looking at question 1, section 4 of the Act says that one 'applies' a trade description by:

- affixing it to, annexing it to, marking it on, or incorporating it with the goods or anything in, on or with which the goods are supplies
- placing the goods in, on or with anything to which the description has been affixed, annexed, etc.
- using the description in any manner which may be taken as referring to the goods.

Question 2 is simple: was what was said true or not?

Then, looking at question 3, would a reasonably objective person reading or hearing the description have been misled?

If you apply this test, it should be obvious that a lie is always a false trade description. If the statement is not a lie, but misleads one into believing that it was true, it is 'false to a material degree' and an offence was probably committed.

WARNING: An oral statement you make can apply a trade description.

WARNING: A customer who uses a trade description when asking for goods can make you liable.

Although the main purpose of the early part of the Act makes it an offence to apply a false trade description you have to consider first of all what is a 'trade description'. The Act says that it is:

- an indication, direct or indirect, and by whatever means given, of any of the following matters with respect to goods or parts of goods ...

and there is a long list of items which are covered:

- quantity, size or gauge
- method of manufacture, production, processing or re-conditioning;
- composition
- fitness for purpose, strength, performance, behaviour or accuracy
- any physical characteristics not included above
- testing by any person and results thereof
- approval by any person or conformity with approved type
- place or date or manufacture, etc.
- person by whom manufactured, etc.
- other history including previous ownership or use.

Note that: 'quantity' includes length, width, height, area, volume, capacity, weight and number.

It is important to note that a trade description can be given 'by any means'. This covers notices in shops, advertisements, statements in any documents handed to a customer as well as anything which might have been said by a sales assistant.

 WARNING: Train staff to understand that they must not say anything about what they are selling unless they know that it is true and accurate.

The list of items may seem to be self-explanatory, but it is amazing how frequently traders say or do something which the courts find to be a 'false trade description'.

Here are some examples:

- An advert containing a picture of ready-assembled furniture which was actually sold 'knocked down' and had to be put together by the customer – *Queensway v. Burke (1985)*.

- A notice outside a shop saying that some computer software included some games which were not available when a customer bought the software – *Denard v. Smith & Dixons (1990)*.

- A national advert which said that a stove top grill would fit 'every

burner – gas, electric or propane' but did not work on a customer's gas cooker – *Janbo Trading v. Dudley MBC (1993)*.

- A watch described as 'waterproof' which stopped after an hour under water – *Sherratt v. Geralds (1970)*.

- A car described as having had 'one owner' when that one owner had in fact leased the car to five different people – *R. v. South Western Justices (1983)*.

- Displaying for sale a 'look-alike' cube puzzle almost identical to the Rubik Cube even though the name was different – *Surrey CC v. Clark (1991)*.

- Telling a customer that he could have identical furniture to that on display where what was supplied was very different – *Cavendish Woodhouse v. Wright (1985)*.

- An advert for a car which said that it was 'in showroom condition throughout' when it had serious faults – *Hawkins v. Smith (1978)*.

There have been hundreds of cases were traders have been convicted for what may seem to be stupid things but which enforcement staff would call deliberate deceptions:

- marking turkeys as 'Norfolk' when they were not
- displaying counterfeit clothes, videos, etc.
- saying that clothes can be 'machine-washed/tumble-dried' but which stretched
- selling an insurance write-off car as 'brand new'
- 'leather' shoes of which only part was real leather.

Misleading containers

Traders have been convicted of offences under the Trade Descriptions Act 1968 for:

- supplying meat in a container giving the appearance of a larger quantity than marked
- using a container for a cosmetic, correctly labelled as to its contents, but with a false bottom; its size and shape misled customers into believing they were getting more than the indicated volume – *R. v. Pears (1982)*.

New goods

To protect ordinary shoppers, the law assumes that – unless clearly marked to the contrary – what is being sold is new. This may seem obvious but it was not until the early 1970s that the Court of Appeal dealt with the principle in *R. v. Ford Motor Co (1973)*. Here a car had been built for export; the order was cancelled. While in transit between the maker and dealer, the car was damaged; the cost of repair was £50. The car passed through several hands and ended up on a garage forecourt where it was sold to a private customer. The court (which threw out the case) laid down a series of tests:

- The goods must not have been previously sold by retail
- They must not have been put to extensive use
- If they had been damaged, what was the nature and extent of the damage and the quality of the repair
- It was not a false use of 'new' if the damage was superficial or limited to defined parts which could be replaced so as to make the article as goods as new.

In a later case, in 1987, a car importer was convicted of selling mint cars as 'new' when they had already been registered – to boost sales figures *(R v. Anderson)*.

There have been many cases where retailers have been convicted. One involved the sale of a television. A customer bought the set, took it home, filled in the guarantee, then found that it would not work. He took it back to the shop which immediately gave him a refund. The television was repaired and tested and put back on sale. A second person bought it in good faith but discovered the completed guarantee card in the packaging. He complained and the trading standards department prosecuted.

In 1993 *(Gale v. Dixons)* a customer bought a computer from a chain store. Although it was assumed to be new, it had been sold to someone else who brought it back complaining about a fault. The company had the computer repaired and put it back on sale without any indication of the history. The store was convicted.

 WARNING: If anything is not 'new', make sure it is clearly marked with its previous history.

 WARNING: Train staff that if they are asked whether goods are new, they must check before answering.

 WARNING: If goods are returned because of faults, don't be tempted to put them back on the shelf as new.

False or misleading statements about services

The second part of the Act tries to control what is said about services. Section 14 of the Trade Descriptions Act 1968 makes it an offence for any person in the course of a business:

- to make a statement which he knows to be false, or
- recklessly to make a statement which is false, about:
 - the provision of, or nature of, services, accommodation or facilities
 - the time at which such services, etc., are provided
 - the manner in which they are provided, or
 - the persons by whom they are provided.

The section says that you commit an offence if the claims that you make about your services are wrong – for example:

- 'same day service' that takes longer than one day
- architect – when you are not qualified as one
- 500 metres from the sea – if it is actually a mile
- builder covered by National House Builders Council scheme – but not true
- issuing an airline ticket for a non-existent flight.

You will be convicted only if the court finds that you knew that the statement was false when you made it or if you made it regardless of whether it was true or false.

 WARNING: Do not claim membership of any trade association or professional body if you are not a member.

 WARNING: Make sure that anything you say about the way you offer services is true (and can be verified).

Advertisements

What has been said above about false trade descriptions and making false statements about services, etc., applies as much to advertisements as to notices in shops.

There is no one Act of Parliament specifically dealing with advertising although many indicate what may or may not be said about activities. As we have already noted (page 24), the British Codes of Advertising and Sales Promotion are voluntary. There is no criminal sanction for a breach.

Disclaimers

Under certain, very limited, circumstances it is possible to 'disclaim' a trade description; that is, you may be able to demonstrate to a court that you took steps to inform shoppers that you were unable to substantiate the description. Disclaimers are often found in the second-hand car trade. The mileage recorded on a vehicle's mileometer is, by its very nature, a trade description because it indicates the history. Because a dealer may not know whether the figure shown is true and accurate or whether the clock was turned back, he may try to nullify it by indicating his ignorance of the truth and the unreliability of the mileage reading.

It is impossible to put any disclaimer to cancel a false trade description which you have applied yourself; therefore you cannot use a disclaimer to avoid a conviction under section 1(1)(a) of the Trade Descriptions Act 1968 (see page 118).

You may be able to disclaim a false description applied by someone else in order to get out of a prosecution under section 1(1)(b) – of 'supplying or offering to supply' goods bearing the false description. However, case law over the years has resulted in a set of rules (see *Norman v. Bennett (1974)*) which you must follow if you hope to be able to convince a court:

- the disclaimer must be as 'bold, precise and compelling' as the false trade description itself
- the disclaimer must be effectively brought to the notice of any customer before any contract is made.

 WARNING: You can never disclaim anything you know to be false.

For example, a motor dealer wound back a clock, then put on a sticker saying that the reading was not guaranteed – guilty (Newman v Hackney (1982))

 WARNING: You can never disclaim a statement you made.

 WARNING: To be legally effective the disclaimer must be as obvious as and in close proximity to the description being avoided.

Due diligence defence

This important defence is available in certain circumstances; it is discussed in Chapter 10.

Restrictive Notices in shops, etc.

Many traders put up notices by which they try to tell would-be customers about their policy on refunds and taking goods back.

As we have seen in earlier chapters, every customer who buys goods from a retailer makes a contract and the Sale of Goods Act 1979 gives the shopper certain rights about the quality and fitness of what is bought – which cannot be taken away.

While there is nothing wrong with simple statements about the way you run the shop – 'no dogs', 'no children', 'no smoking' – once you try to indicate that customers' rights are reduced you will fall foul of the Consumer Transactions (Restrictions on Statements) Order 1976. This Order deals with two situations which have some impact on retailers who sell goods to customer:

- You must not indicate – by any notice, advertisement or document – that the civil rights of a genuine complainant are excluded. This covers such statements as:
 - 'No cash refunds'
 - 'All umbrellas must be checked before leaving till. No returns can be accepted'

- 'All sale goods bought as seen. No refunds or exchanges'
- 'No sale goods exchanged or money refunded'
- 'Sold as seen and approved'
- 'Sold without any warranty'
- 'Sold as scrap'
- 'As seen, tried and approved'
- 'Purchased as seen'.

- You may only make a statement that has a possible effect on customers' rights, if it is accompanied by another 'clear and conspicuous' statement 'in close proximity' saying:

 'Your statutory rights are not affected.'

This means that statements such as 'Refunds will only be made within 28 days of purchase' or 'Sale goods may only be returned if defective' must have the additional wording.

 WARNING: Do not put up any notice or have any written contract term which denies customers their right to get refunds for defective goods.

 WARNING: Even using this qualification, you may still commit an offence. Take legal advice before putting up any notice or drafting a contract term.

Price Promotions

Many older traders will remember that the principal rules about prices were set out in the Trade Descriptions Act 1968 and in various Orders. These were all scrapped in 1989 when a new regime came into force under Part III of the Consumer Protection Act 1987.

Under section 20 of the 1987 Act it is an offence for any trader to give consumers – by any means:

- an indication which is misleading as to the price at which any goods, services, accommodation or facilities are available.

It is also an offence to continue to display a price indication which, although not misleading when first given, has become so, and consumers might be misled.

What does 'misleading' mean?

Often it will be quite obvious that the price indicated is incorrect. In such a case, there is no doubt that it is misleading. To help in less blatant cases, section 21 of the 1987 Act says that a price indication is 'misleading' if it leads consumers to believe:

- the price is less than it really is

or any of the following:

- the price does not have any strings attached
- there are no hidden extras
- that a price reduction will last a given time (when it does not)
- that a price increase will start on a certain date (when it does not)
- that a price comparison is valid (when it is not).

when the actual position is different.

Similar rules apply where what is indicated is not the price itself but a method of working out a price.

The Act applies not only to prices for goods and things which are obvious services, but extends to cover banking, foreign exchange,

electricity supply, off-street parking and caravan parks (other than permanent homes). It also applies to the sale of new houses, either sold freehold or on leases of at least 21 years.

Code of Practice

In order to help traders understand the way price marking is supposed to work, the Act gave the Minister power to draw up a Code of Practice. This document should be on the desk of every retailer. It is called the Code of Practice for Traders on Price Indications and is available from HMSO. It spells out in straightforward language what you may and may not do when indicating prices generally, and when making reductions.

- Don't use words or phrases which suggest a price comparison if you are not making one.
- When making a reduction, always show the previous higher price;
- Always make clear what the previous higher price was.
- 'Reduced from £...' should always refer to your own previous price.
- Don't use initials or abbreviations to describe the higher price; the only permitted use is 'RRP' or 'man. rec. price'.
- Don't use 'worth' or 'value' claims.
- Don't say that something is 'free' if you make a charge for it; or have inflated the basic price to cover, say postage and delivery, or if you will reduce the price to customers who do not take up the free item.
- All prices quoted to consumers should include VAT; for business customers, VAT-exclusive prices are allowed, but if there are also private shoppers it must be clear whether or not VAT is payable.

Comparisons

When you are comparing with your own prices, follow these rules:

- The previous price should have been the last one at which goods were available for customers in the previous six months.
- The goods should have been available at that price for at least 28 consecutive days in the last six months.
- The previous price should have applied at the same shop where the reduction is being made.

If you are unable to meet any of these simple requirements, give a clear and positive explanation – as prominent as the price indication – about the period and circumstances relating to the higher price.

Here are some useful tips:

- *Don't* use a general disclaimer that the 28 day rule does not apply.
- *Don't* call a promotion an introductory offer unless it is intended to offer the goods after the offer period is over and at a higher price.
- *Don't* let offers run on and on.
- *Only* indicate an 'after-sale' price if you are certain that the price will be applied and held for at least 28 days in the three months after the sale ends.
- *Don't* use 'ASP' or 'APP'.
- *Don't* use 'RAP' to mean 'ready-assembled price' especially when goods are not normally available in that state anyway (see page 120, Queensway case).

Other comparisons are allowed:

- with goods in different circumstances
- different prices for quantity
- 'when perfect'
- for goods in a different state
- for groups of people.

The Act says that following the Code is not an absolute defence, but it will tend to show that you have not committed an offence.

Bar-coding – pitfalls

Many pricing errors occur when shelf-edge prices are lower than those contained in central computer data-bases searched by scanners reading barcodes. Worse, when a mistake is pointed out by puzzled customers, checkout staff may blame 'the computer' and claim that there is really nothing that can be done to prevent this sort of error. A wrong bar-code on a whole batch means that all the prices will be wrong with potentially ghastly results for you.

There is no excuse. The price muddle is a classic example of a 'misleading indication'. When a customer sees a shelf-edge price of 55p,

chooses the goods on that basis but is told at the till that the price is 'really' 62p, and is told that it is the computer's fault and the higher price must be charged, then you cannot blame him for reporting the matter to the Trading Standards department.

 WARNING: Tell all checkout staff that whenever there is a discrepancy between a shelf price and the scanned price, the customer should be charged the lower price and an apology given.

 WARNING: It may be better sometimes to withdraw the goods from sale at that moment (if, for example, a £99 item is indicated as £0.99)

The sense of this was underlined in *Toys 'R' Us v. Gloucestershire County Council (1994)* when the Court of Appeal held that there was no offence when goods bore a price ticket but the trader's bar-code scanning system revealed a higher price, because the prudent trader has a policy of always charging the lower ticket price. This is also something to be considered when seeing whether the 'due diligence' defence can be invoked (see Chapter 10).

Other rules about price marking

Price Marking (Food and Drink on Premises) Order 1979

This applies to all places where food is sold to the public except:

- clubs; works' or office canteens, schools
- premises where food only supplied to people who have sleeping accommodation

and says that anyone who sells food must:

- give an indication of the price of the food, and
- indicate any extra charge (e.g. service charge or corkage)
- indicate that VAT is inclusive.

On the price list, the seller must show the price of:

- all types of food up to 30 categories, or
- if the list is divided into categories –
 - up to five types of each food

- up to six types of table wine (if sold)
- up to two types of red, white and rosé wine.

Price Indications (Method of Payment) Regulations 1991

Until this law, traders had to charge the same price for goods and services whether the customer paid by cash or cheque or used a credit card.

Now – but not for motor fuel – it is possible to impose differential charges so long as would-be customers are given clear information about what you are doing before they contemplate making a contract with you.

This can be done either orally – by telling the customer audibly – or by displaying an easily identifiable notice, clearly and unambiguously expressing your pricing policy. The written notice must be displayed:

- at each public entrance
- at each checkout or pay-point where customers have to pay
- at any filling-station shop
- at any car-park
- at the entrance of any 'shop within a shop'
- on any kiosk, stall, booth, etc.
- on all menus
- in any form of transport
- in any mail-order or telephone-order advert.

Price Marking Order 1999

This Order implements European Union Directives and says that:

- where a person indicates that any goods (apart from motor fuel) are for sale by retail, the selling price must be indicated in an unambiguous and easily identifiable manner clearly legible by a prospective purchaser.

This may be done in several ways:

- where goods can be seen:
 - on the goods, or
 - on a ticket or notice displayed on, or
 - grouped with other prices on the list near the goods;

- where goods are not on show:
 - in an advertisement
 - on the goods, or

- if they are prepacked – on the container, or
- in a catalogue or price list on a VDU

and the price must be inclusive of the current VAT rate.

Note that there was a court case (*Allen v. Redbridge London Borough Council (1993)*) concerning a retail chemist who stocked a wide range of perfumes in a large, locked glass cabinet. Price labels were placed at the bottom of or on the back of the boxes in which the perfumes were contained, and a potential purchaser could find the price only by asking a salesperson to unlock the cabinet and remove items for closer examination.

The prosecution argued that the Price Marking Order said that a would-be buyer, looking at an article for sale, wherever it was in the shop, had to be able to see the price without asking for help.

The appeal court rejected that argument and held that the Order was fully complied with provided there was on the article, clearly stated by whatever means, or alongside it some indicator unmistakably referring to it, showing the price. There was no requirement for a retailer to put the price label on the front of an article or to put the goods in a position where they could be handled by a prospective buyer. It was enough that assistance from someone in the shop enabled the buyer to see the price.

So there is now judicial authority that it is reasonable for a prospective shopper to have to ask about prices.

- Where a customer has to pay for postage, package or delivery, the price of those extras must be unambiguous, easily identifiable and clearly legible.

A huge range of goods (liquid foods, solid foods and non-foods) set out in the First Schedule to the Order will have to be unit priced unless:

- the unit price is identical to the selling price
- they are pre-packed in a constant quantity and sold in a small shop, by an itinerant trader or from a vending machine
- they are offered in a radio, TV or cinema advert
- the goods are damaged, deteriorating or in an assortment.

Due diligence defence

This important defence is available in cases involving price marking offences (see Chapter 10).

Origin marking

There used to be a law in this country (the Trade Descriptions Act 1972) which required many imported goods which had been given a British name or mark to carry a note of their country of origin. In 1988, this law was repealed because its purpose had been challenged by the European Commission. It was said that origin marking discriminated against goods from other Member States.

A new order was brought into force from 1 January 1989. The Trade Descriptions (Place of Production) (Marking) Order 1988 imposes a duty on manufacturers (and retailers) to give indications of origin on certain types of goods which carry what might otherwise be misleading marks. The Order was aimed in part at the Japanese-sounding name of a UK-manufactured electronic product (so called because the maker presumably thought that British customers might be more likely to buy his product if they thought it was made in Japan).

The Order says that:

- where goods available for sale or supply by retail are presented in such a way that a misleading indication as to where they were manufactured is given, they must be marked with or accompanied by a statement of their real origin, i.e. the place (not necessarily the *country*).

There is also a list of matters to be considered when judging whether there has been a misleading mark. These include:

- names, images, emblems, flags, devices, references to or representations of things (like buildings or geographical features), or to or of persons living, dead or fictional.

So, if a UK manufacturer made a suite of French-style furniture and marked it with an Eiffel Tower, he would have to include 'Made in Britain' because otherwise it might be thought to have been made in France.

Watch out for the following:

- If a marking is required by UK or EU law the rules can be disregarded.
- Do company or brand names include any place name (High Wycombe, Worcester Park, Morden), or refer to anyone (Bonnie Prince Charlie, perhaps) or show the Rockies. Do they contain a

flag, logo or national symbol?
● Are they accompanied by an address which is not in the country where they were made?

If goods are marked with any of these but not produced in the place associated with the name, etc., there must be a clear statement where they were made.

Two other orders are in force.

The Trade Descriptions (Sealskin Goods) (Information) Order 1980 says that:

● products made from sealskin must be marked with that fact and where the sealskin came from (country or geographical area).

The Trade Descriptions Act 1968 says that the country of origin shall be the place in which goods last underwent a treatment resulting in a 'substantial change'. The Trade Descriptions (Country of Origin) (Cutlery) Order 1981, which was brought in to protect UK cutlery manufacturing, says that:

● silver-plating of cutlery does not result in 'substantial change'.

Therefore all cutlery made abroad but plated in the UK must be marked with the country where the cutlery itself was made.

Textile Fibre Content

To many people's surprise, the familiar care label which appears on most garments has no statutory basis. It is entirely voluntary and arises from the membership of the Home Laundering Consultative Council of the International Textile Care Labelling Association.

However, the Textile Products (Indication of Fibre Content) Regulations 1986 make manufacturers (and retailers) responsible for ensuring that the vast majority of the following 'textile products' are clearly and legibly marked or labelled in English with an indication of the content of all fibres comprised in the products:

● raw, semi-worked, worked, semi-manufactured, manufactured, semi-made-up or made-up products which are exclusively composed of textile fibres, regardless of the mixing or assembly process employed

- products containing not less than 80 per cent by weight of textile fibres
- furniture, umbrella and sunshade coverings containing not less than 80 per cent by weight of textile fibres
- the textile parts of multi-layer floor-coverings, of mattresses and of camping goods, and the warm linings of footwear, gloves, mittens and mitts if such parts and linings contain not less than 80 per cent by weight of textile fibres.

Part I of Schedule 2 of the regulations lays down a list of some 50 names which must be used to identify fibres; they must be shown in descending order of proportion.

 WARNING: Only goods made entirely of only one fibre may be marked '100%', 'pure' or 'all' (though up to 5 per cent of others are allowed in certain circumstances).

There are special rules where there are two or more fibres making up at least 85 per cent and for the use of the expressions 'other fibres' and 'mixed fibres'.

There is a list in Schedule 4 of 43 miscellaneous items – ranging from coffee cosies and tobacco pouches to animal clothing, flags and banners – which are formally exempted from the labelling rules.

Schedule 5 contains a list of small items – from children's ties, floor clothes to curtain tape – where only one fibre need be marked, so long as the actual information is 'easily accessible' to the customer.

 WARNING: There are frequent prosecutions for wrong labels; make sure that you know your supplier; make him give you full technical details.

Due diligence defence

This important defence is available in many consumer protection offences (see Chapter 10).

Penalties

If you are found guilty, the penalties are:

- in a magistrates' court – a fine up to £5,000 per offence
- in the Crown Court – an unlimited fine and/or up to two years in prison.

Weights and Measures

Legal controls of weighing and measuring equipment and the sale of goods by quantity are amongst the oldest of consumer protection laws.

Before being used for trade purposes all petrol pumps, scales, weights, capacity measures, length measures, etc., must be examined and tested by an inspector. The equipment will bear a mark to show that it has passed the tests.

Retailers have a duty to ensure that their equipment is maintained in good order in order to avoid any possibility of it becoming false or unjust.

Similarly, steps should be taken to prevent any short weight or short measure being delivered to a customer when goods are being sold by quantity.

Since 1979, the UK has adopted the 'average quantity' system for many pre-packed goods but this is unlikely to be relevant to retailers who will only be concerned with goods that they weigh or measure on their own premises. Apart from some allowances for normal packaging, these sales will be by minimum weight.

More recently, legislation has been introduced which makes the use of metric units compulsory in the vast majority of transactions for foods and non-foods. There are a few exemptions – for instance, the pint is retained for draught beer and cider, and for milk in bottles.

Prohibited sales to children

It is a criminal offence to sell certain things to young people. Here is a list of some of the most common:

Cigarettes	under 16
Crossbows	under 17
Firearms – sale	under 17
– gift/loan	under 14
Gift or loan of shotgun	under 15
Fireworks	under 16
Gunpowder	under 16
Harmful solvents ('sniffing')	under 18
'Horror comics'	under 18
Intoxicating liquor	under 18
Lottery tickets/scratch cards	under 16

Pet animals	under 12
Taking pawns	under 14
Tattooing (unless by doctor)	under 18
Tobacco	under 16
Videos with age classification various	up to 18

 WARNING: Although there is often a defence that you had reasonable grounds for believing the youngster to be over the age limit, it is far better to ensure that you and all your staff apply this rule: when in doubt – don't.

Summary of Key Learning Points

1. *Breaking the criminal law – however inadvertently – can have expensive consequences; make sure you keep up to date with changes and have skilled legal advice on anything which you do not understand.*

2. *If anyone complains that information is wrong, an advertisement is misleading or a label inaccurate – <u>do not argue</u>. Offer a refund.*

3. *An oral statement you make can apply a trade description.*

4. *A customer who uses a trade description when asking for goods can make you liable.*

5. *Train staff to understand that they must <u>not</u> say anything about what they are selling unless they know that it is true and accurate.*

6. *If anything is not 'new', make sure it is clearly marked with its previous history.*

7. *Train staff that if they are asked whether goods are new, they must check before answering.*

8. *If goods are returned because of faults, <u>don't</u> be tempted to put them back on the shelf as new.*

9. *Do not claim membership of any trade association or professional body if you are not a member.*

10. *Make sure that anything you say about the way you offer services is true (and can be verified).*

11. *You can never disclaim anything you <u>know</u> to be false.*

12. *You can never disclaim a statement you made.*

13. *To be legally effective a disclaimer must be as obvious as and in close proximity to the description being avoided.*

14. *Do not put up any notice or have any written contract term which denies customers their right to get refunds for defective goods.*

15. *Even using a qualification, you may still commit an offence. Take legal advice <u>before</u> putting up any notice or drafting a contract term.*

16. *Tell all checkout staff that whenever there is a discrepancy between a shelf price and the scanned price, the customer should be charged the lower price AND given an apology.*

Summary of Key Learning Points

17. It may be better sometimes to withdraw the goods from sale at that moment (if, for example, a £99 item is indicated as £0.99).

18. Only goods made entirely of only one fibre may be marked '100%', 'pure' or 'all' (though up to 5% of others are allowed in certain circumstances).

19. There are frequent prosecutions for wrong labels. Make sure that you know your supplier; make him give you full technical details.

20. Although there is often a defence that you had reasonable grounds for believing a youngster to be over the age limit, it is far better to ensure that you and all your staff apply this rule: when in doubt – <u>don't</u>.

Checklist

☞ Do we check the accuracy of information in advertisements, labels and tickets? Who has the job of checking - and who checks the checkers?

☞ How do we ensure that all staff give accurate information and describe goods correctly?

☞ Do we ensure that "returned" or "faulty" goods are checked and repaired before being put back on sale? Are they correctly labelled as not being new? Who does this? Do they understand why?

☞ Do any disclaimer notices comply with the rules? Are they bold and prominent? Who checks this?

☞ Are our price promotion indications accurate and legal? What action do we need to take?

☞ Do we have a copy of the Code of Practice on Price Indications? Where is it? Do we follow it to the letter? Have we taken legal advice on it? Who is responsible for ensuring that it is followed? Who trains the staff about using the Code and what happens if they do not?

☞ How do we avoid discrepancies between bar-coding and shelf-edge prices? Do branch and department managers understand the need to keep the prices accurate all the time?

☞ Do we sell food? If so, do our pricing policies comply with the rules?

☞ Do all our goods comply with origin marking requirements? What action do we take to ensure that our suppliers comply?

☞ Who is responsible for checking the accuracy of labels on goods - especially garments where fibre content is vital?

☞ Do the sales staff know and understand what cannot be sold to children? How and when are they trained and by whom?

8

Criminal Law: Safety And Food

There are two legal aspects of safety: criminal liability and civil responsibility. As we have been looking at crime in the previous chapter, we shall start with the way in which the criminal law imposes duties on traders about safety.

Safety regulations – old style

For many years there have been safety regulations which made it illegal to sell certain types of goods unless they conformed to British Standards. The goods still covered by regulations made under the Consumer Protection Act 1961 (now repealed) are:

- carry-cot stands
- cooking utensils
- pencils and graphic instruments
- children's clothing (hood cords)
- prams and pushchairs.

There was no power to take goods off the market and the list was relatively small. Changes were made in 1978 which enabled the Government to make orders banning the supply of unsafe goods and requiring public warnings to be given.

The 'general safety requirement'

In 1987, a completely new legal approach was introduced. Part II of the Consumer Protection Act 1987 makes it an offence:

- to supply any consumer goods which fail to
- comply with the 'general safety requirement'

- to offer or agree to supply any such goods
- to expose or possess any such goods for supply.

'Consumer goods' are those which are ordinarily intended for private use or consumption (excluding, among others, cars, drugs and tobacco, because they are controlled by other laws).

The Act goes on to say that consumer goods fail the 'general safety requirement' if:

- they are not reasonably safe having regard to all the circumstances, including:
 - how the goods are marketed
 - their get-up
 - the use of any mark
 - instructions and warnings about their keeping, use or consumption
 - any relevant safety standards
 - whether the goods could have been made safer (taking cost and extent of improvement into account).

Obviously a great deal will turn on the meaning of 'safe', which the Act defines as meaning:

- that there is no risk, or one reduced to a minimum, that death or personal injury will be caused to anyone by:
 - the goods
 - the keeping, use or consumption of the goods
 (a) by people. and
 (b) in conjunction with other goods
 - their assembly
 - emission or leakage from the goods
 - reliance on the accuracy of any goods.

 WARNING: The 'general safety requirement' applies to everything that you sell – not merely goods covered by former regulations.

It is a defence to any proceedings against you for selling goods which do not meet the general safety requirement that:

- you believed they would not be used in the UK

- you had no reasonable grounds for believing that they failed to comply
- the goods were second-hand.

Safety regulations – new style

In addition, the 1987 Act enables specific safety regulations to be made laying down standards for goods. The following table contains a list of the current ones:

- cosmetic products
- furniture and furnishings
- ceramic ware
- gas appliances
- low-voltage electrical equipment
- toys
- fireguards
- implantable medical devices
- child-resistant packaging
- plugs and sockets.

Defence of due diligence

This important defence is available (see Chapter 10).

Penalties

If you are found guilty of selling (or simply possessing or offering to sell) goods which do not meet the 'general safety requirement' or for a breach of any safety regulations the penalties are:

- in a magistrates court – a fine of up to £5,000 and/or up to six months in prison.

Other regulations

A brand new set of rules came into force on October 3, 1994. The General Product Safety Regulations 1994 ('GPSR') implement an EU Directive. What is their effect and how do they square with existing UK product safety legislation?

The GPSR are rather confusing since they also talk of a 'general safety requirement', the requirements of which are considered below. One good

thing is that you cannot be prosecuted under the Consumer Protection Act and the GPSR for the same activity.

The GPSR have two aims. The first is to make it an offence for a producer to:

- place an unsafe product on the market
- 'producer' is defined as:
 - the manufacturer (if he is established in the EU)
 - anyone who appears to be manufacturer because his name, trade or other distinctive mark is on the product
 - the importer (if the manufacturer does not have an established representative in the EU)
 - otherwise, the manufacturer's representative,

all of which are perfectly recognisable. However, there is an additional category which one can see at once could cause problems:

 - *other professionals in the supply chain insofar as their activities may affect the safety properties of a product placed on the market.*

These people are clearly not ordinary retailers (who are covered by Regulation 9, where they are given their own responsibilities). Presumably, by reference to the 'supply chain', the intention is to catch anyone who assembles, installs or services a product: would a car dealer carrying out a pre-delivery inspection come within scope rather than a designer or worker in a factory?

- 'Product' is defined as any product – new, used or reconditioned – intended for, or likely to be used by, consumers (whether it is sold or given away) supplied in the course of a 'commercial activity' (which includes a business and a trade).

To see whether a product is caught by the Consumer Protection Act 1987, one has to look at its ordinarily intended purpose before supply. Under the GPSR one looks at the purpose for which it will be used by an individual purchaser. Therefore, when a person supplies a professional product to a consumer, which he believes is likely to be used by that consumer, the product comes within the GPSR.

It is logical, therefore, that the 1994 regulations should apply a similar exclusive test. Also excluded are:

- second-hand products sold as 'antiques'
- those supplied for repair or reconditioning before use provided the buyer is clearly informed, or
- any product whose safety is already covered by specific EU laws governing safety.

The third point means that where there are rules in EU law which govern all aspects of the safety of the product (e.g. toys) the GPSR do not apply. However, they will apply to safety aspects of a product which are regulated under EU law in part. For example, a food imitation with a sharp edge likely to cut a child will be subject to the GPSR. They also apply to products regulated by UK regulations not implementing an EU directive; so domestic upholstered furniture is subject to both the existing UK regulations and the GPSR.

Duty to supply information

In contrast to the 1987 Act position, where compliance with the general safety requirement may be measured in terms of instructions or warnings supplied with the goods, Regulation 8 of the 1994 regulations imposes a duty on producers:

- to provide information to enable consumers to assess risks inherent in the product throughout its expected life and take precautions
- to monitor risks and have a product recall mechanism. This may be done by marking product batches, doing sample testing, investigating complaints and keeping retailers informed.

New duties for retailers

What is your position as a retailer? The regulations call retailers 'distributors' – those in the supply chain whose activity does not affect the safety properties of the product. You must take note of information received from suppliers, customers, media reports and enforcement agencies about the safety of products.

Where there are reasonable grounds to believe that a product is dangerous, you are best advised to withdraw it from sale until the matter has been investigated.

 WARNING: You will be convicted if you sell an unsafe product and you failed to cooperate and remove it from sale.

You must take part in monitoring the safety of goods by passing on to your customers information on risks and on the action taken to avoid them.

Are products safe?

The 1994 regulations contain a presumption that if a product conforms with existing mandatory health and safety requirements, it is safe. Where there are no existing safety rules, conformity to safety is to be measured by reference to:

- voluntary UK standards giving effect to a European standard
- EU technical specifications
- where there are neither of the above –
 (a) UK standards, or
 (b) relevant codes of practice, or
 (c) state of the art and technology, and the safety which consumers may readily expect.

Compliance with a harmonised safety standard gives the supplier an assurance that the product meets the relevant safety requirements.

Definition of 'safe'

The 1994 regulations say that a product is safe if:

- under normal or reasonably foreseeable conditions of use, including duration, it does not present any risk or only a minimum risk compatible with a high level of protection.
- Account shall be taken of:
 - the characteristics of the product, including: composition, packaging, assembly instructions, maintenance
 - its effect on other products
 - presentation, labelling, instructions for use and disposal
 - groups particularly at risk, particularly children.

The fact that higher levels of safety could be available will not of itself result in the product being treated as unsafe.

Prohibition notices and notices to warn

The Consumer Protection Act 1987 contains powers for the following to be made:

- **'prohibition notices'** – which ban the supply of any goods specified in the notice
- **'notices to warn'** – which require the trader who is served (usually, but not always, the manufacturer or importer) to publish information about goods which are considered to be unsafe
- **'suspension notices'** – which ban the person served from supplying any specified goods without consent
- **'forfeiture orders'** may be applied for at magistrates' courts if goods fail the general safety requirement or there has been a prohibition or suspension notice. The court can also order their destruction.

Product recall

Although there is no statutory provision in the UK for product recall, enforcement authorities are under a duty to inform the Secretary of State about any action they take to remove dangerous products from sale. This may lead to EU-wide action.

 WARNING: Never ignore advice from enforcement officers about dangerous products.

Flammability

This is an extremely important issue for anyone selling furniture. There are detailed rules set out in the Furniture and Furnishings (Fire)(Safety) Regulations 1988 (which have been amended twice since then) and you should have a copy of the regulations and any guidance from your trade association and the industry. In summary they say that:

- No furniture (other than mattresses, bed-bases, pillows and cushions) may include upholstery which does not pass the 'cigarette test' in BS 5852 Part I (modified in respect of invisible parts of permanent covers).

● No furniture (other than pillows and cushions) may include any filling material which fails the relevant ignitability test, and no furniture may include as a filling any crumb foam which is not derived from combustion-modified foam.

● For loose-filling material for pillows, cushions or upholstering or re-upholstering furniture, polyurethane foam in slab or cushion form must meet the test in Schedule 1, Part I (BS 5852 Part II); crumb foam is not allowed; latex foam must meet the test in Schedule 1, Part III.

● Permanent covers for furniture (except mattresses, bed- bases, cushions and pillows) must meet the 'match test' in Schedule 5, Part III. The cover or fabric intended to replace the permanent cover on such furniture must pass the 'match test' or have an interliner made from specified material (at least 75 per cent of cotton, flax, viscose, modal, silk or wool used separately or together and not coated with polyurethane).
 • Insulated bags for carrying babies under six months are excluded.

● Covers, other than permanent covers, for furniture except mattresses, bed-bases, cushions and pillows, must pass the appropriate 'match test' – for loose covers, that in Schedule 5, Part I; for stretch covers, Schedule 5, Part II.

● 'Caution' swing labels must be attached to furniture, except mattresses, bed-bases, cushions and pillows displayed in shops; they must be attached so as to be clearly visible and so that the back and front can be read with as little inconvenience as possible.

● All furniture and covers (apart from mattresses and bed-bases) must carry permanent labels as set out in Schedule 7 saying 'carelessness causes fires' and other details.

● Any manufacturer, importer or retailer of most foam-filled furniture must be able to tell a trading standards officer:
 • who made the furniture
 • date of manufacture or import
 • details of fillings and coverings
 • test results and records.

● All manufacturers and importers must give information about the result of prescribed tests to enable the regulations to be enforced in

respect of furniture except mattresses, bed-bases, cushions and pillows.

- From 1 January 1997, second-hand furniture which is hired out at the same time as and in connection with the letting of accommodation must meet most of the regulations.

- The supply of any furniture which does not comply with the regulations is prohibited, except when it is part of the fixtures and fittings of a second-hand caravan.

Defence of due diligence
This important defence is available (see Chapter 10).

Claims of non-inflammability
There may be textiles which are advertised and sold as being non-inflammable or safe from fire. By the Fabrics (Misdescription) Regulations 1959:

- claims that textile fabric is non-inflammable or safe from fire
 — allowed if fabric meets test under BS 3119 and washed in accordance with BS 3120 both before and after flame test.

- similar claims about fabric made up into garment
 — allowed if garment meets BS 3119.

- claims that textile fabric is non-inflammable or safe from fire
 — allowed if fabric meets vertical strip test under BS 2963 and washed in accordance with BS 3121 both before and after flame test.

By the Fabrics (Misdescription) Regulations 1980:

- claims that textile fabric- to cigarettes or lighted matches
 — allowed if fabric meets resistant smouldering cigarette test or butane flame test.

Stop Now Orders

The Stop Now Orders (EC Directive) Regulations 2001 enables action to

be taken against a trader who is believed to be in breach of any of the following regulations:

- Control of Misleading Advertisements Regulations 1988

- Consumer Protection (Cancellation of Contracts Concluded away from Business Premises) Regulations 1987

- Consumer Credit Act 1974

- Package Travel, Package Holidays and Package Tours Regulations 1992

- Medicines (Advertising) Regulations 1994

- Unfair Terms in Consumer Contracts Regulations 1999

- Timeshare Act 1992

- Consumer Protection (Distance Selling) Regulations 2000

- Sale and Supply of Goods to Consumers Regulations 2002.

The Regulations replace Part III of the Fair Trading Act 1973 which provided a means of dealing with traders who persist in a course of conduct which breaches civil or criminal law in a way which is detrimental to the interests of consumers. The Director General of Fair Trading could ask the court to order the trader to refrain from that course of conduct.

The Stop Now Regulations allow the Director General of Fair Trading, Trading Standards officers and a range of other public bodies to bring proceedings under the Fair Trading Act if there is a breach of one of the above regulations. The new rules remove the existing requirement that before bringing proceedings under this section the Director General must first try to obtain a satisfactory written assurance from the trader that he will refrain from continuing that course of conduct or a similar one.

Unless the Director General considers that circumstances justify immediate proceedings, the trader must be given the opportunity to stop the infringement without the need for court action. If the infringement is not stopped within two weeks after the request for consultation is received, action may be taken without further delay.

If the Court is satisfied that the trader has engaged in conduct which breaks the regulations or is likely to do so, it may make a Stop Now Order which requires the trader to stop the infringement or not to engage in the

conduct which would constitute an infringement. The court may also order the publication of the decision to make the order.

These regulations will be replaced by the application in due course, of s.210 of the Enterprise Act 2002, but the principle set out here remain the same.

Food Safety Act 1990

This Act contains most of the basic legal rules that retailers should know about. In addition there is a range of codes of practice prepared to help both the public and enforcement authorities understand what has to be done. In essence, premises used for the preparation, production, sale, storage and transportation of food and sale of food must at least meet minimum standards of hygiene. The food itself must:

- be fit for human consumption
- be safe to eat
- be of acceptable quality
- be properly described, and
- be honestly labelled and advertised.

Definitions of food, business, commercial operations, etc.

The Act says that 'food' includes:

- drink (including bottled water but not tap water – which is covered by the Food Hygiene Regulations 1995)
- articles and substances of no nutritional value which are used for human consumption
- chewing gum and other products of a like nature and use
- articles and substances used as ingredients in the preparation of food or anything within the above definition.

It does not include:

- live animals or birds or live fish which are not used for human consumption while they are alive
- fodder or feeding stuff for animals, birds or fish
- articles or substances used only as drugs.

There are a series of linked definitions designed to ensure that virtually all

activities connected with food – except those carried out in one's home – come within the Act, its substantive provisions and subordinate legislation to be made under powers contained in the Act. For example,

- 'business' includes a canteen, club, school, hospital or institution – whether or not carried on for profit – and any activity by a public or local authority
- 'food business' means any business in which commercial operations to food or food sources are carried out
- 'food source' means any growing crop or live animal, bird or fish from which food is intended to be derived – by harvesting, slaughtering, milking, collecting eggs, etc.
- 'food premises' means any premises used for a food business
- 'premises' includes any place, vehicle, stall or moveable structure (and may extend to ship or aircraft)
- 'commercial operation' means in relation to food or contact material:
 - selling and possessing, offering, exposing or advertising for sale
 - consigning, delivering or serving for sale
 - preparing, presenting, labelling or wrapping for sale
 - storing, transporting for the purpose of sale
 - importing and exporting
 - deriving food from a food source
- 'contact material' means anything intended to come into contact with food.

This means that selling food in canteens, clubs or other places (see 'business' above) will amount to a 'food business' carrying on 'commercial operations'.

The Act also says that:

- the supply of food – otherwise than on sale – in the course of a business shall be deemed to be a sale.

Thus, food provided free in hospitals, schools or in canteens comes within the Act, which also applies to any food which is offered as a prize or reward or is given away in connection with any entertainment to which the public are admitted, whether or not they had to pay.

Section 3 of the Act contains certain presumptions:

- that food commonly used for human consumption
 - if sold, offered, exposed or kept for sale, or
 - found on premises used for the preparation, storage or sale of that food,
- and any article or substance commonly used in the manufacture of food for human consumption found on such premises,

was intended for sale for human consumption.

Offences against public safety

The Act's main provisions concerning safety and consumer protection are set out in Part II.

Rendering food injurious

By section 7, it is an offence:

- to render food injurious to health by doing any of the following:
 - adding any article or substance
 - using any article or substance as an ingredient
 - abstracting any constituent
 - subjecting it to any other process or treatment and, in looking at the injury to health, regard shall be had not only to the probable effect of the food on the consumer but also its cumulative effect on a person's health.

Food is 'injurious to health' if it affects a substantial number of people; but it does not have to be injurious to everyone. Thus, pregnant women and children represent a 'substantial portion' of the population, and if there was a foodstuff which, when treated in some way, was likely to harm anyone in those two groups, there would be an offence. However, if only exceptional people, such as those with rare allergies, were likely to be harmed, it is improbable that there would be an offence under this section.

Breaching 'food safety requirements'

Section 8 of the Act created a second, new offence:

- to sell food, or to offer, expose or advertise it for sale, or
- to be in possession of food, or

- to deposit or consign the food to anyone for the purpose of such sale or of preparation for sale

which does not comply with 'food safety requirements'.

Food will not meet 'food safety requirements' if:

- it has been rendered injurious to health as a result of anything done in contravention of section 7, or
- it is unfit for human consumption, or
- it is so contaminated (whether by extraneous matter or otherwise) that it would not be reasonable to expect it to be used for human consumption.

This last provision is new and makes it clear that food can now be considered to be unsuitable for human consumption because of serious contamination.

Batches of food

A new presumption is also contained in section 8 that where part of a batch, lot or consignment of food is found to be unsafe, the whole of the batch shall be deemed unsafe unless the contrary is proved. Injury to health is defined as including any permanent or temporary impairment.

Basic legal duties

Section 14 of the Act makes it an offence:

- to sell to the purchaser's prejudice food not of the nature or substance or quality demanded.

A long line of legal cases has decided that 'purchaser' includes a relative, guest, employee or simply a person who consumes the food.

False presentation of food

Section 15 says that it is an offence:

- to sell food which is falsely described or presented in a label whether or not attached to or printed on any wrapper or container, or
- to be concerned with the publication of an advertisement which falsely describes any food or is likely to mislead as to its nature or substance or quality
- to sell, offer, expose for sale, or to be in possession for the purpose

of sale any food the presentation of which is likely to mislead as to its nature or quality or substance.

Breaching food regulations

The 'nuts and bolts' of food law setting out how you must carry on any activity concerning food safety, food preparation, handling, storage, labelling, transport, hygiene and sale are set out in a huge range of detailed regulations made under the Food Safety Act. They cover such things as:

- prohibiting or regulating ingredients used in the composition of food – this will enable restrictions to be placed on the use of additives
- controlling the sale or manufacture of food from any food source (see definition) which may have a specified disease – this will allow controls on the use of live animals which have been treated in such a way that there is a danger to human health from veterinary residues
- regulating the treatment and disposal of unfit food
- requiring food processing to comply with advice from experts and the issue of licences in respect of any process or treatment – it is under this provision that regulations have been drafted in connection with the licensing of food irradiation plants
- making provision for food hygiene at food premises, food businesses, cleansing areas and refuse disposal
- for the training of everyone engaged in any way as food handlers – whether proprietors or employees
- for requiring owners or occupiers of premises to comply with hygiene regulations
- to provide for the inspection of food sources to see if they comply with regulations under the Act and the food safety requirements
- regarding the labelling of food – as in the case of the proposed regulations covering the labelling of food which has been subject to irradiation
- providing for the regulation of materials intended to come into contact with food at any stage in its production.

Food law contains many detailed requirements which are far beyond the scope of this book. There are special rules about meat, dairy products and

milk and others cover all aspects of food treatment from raw materials to ingredients and additives. Regulations deal with anything from bottled water to sardines.

Anyone thinking about starting a food business or adding food to an existing operation must take skilled professional advice. You should also get in touch with the Environmental Health department of your local authority for help and information because all food businesses must be registered with the local authority.

We shall just look at a few of the regulations which retailers who sell food as a side-line should know about.

 WARNING: all food businesses must be registered with the local authority.

Food irradiation

This is a controversial area and there are regulations saying what can be irradiated. The Food (Control of Irradiation) Regulations 1990 say that only the following can be treated by irradiation:

- fruit (including fungi, tomatoes and rhubarb)
- vegetables (including pulses)
- cereals
- bulbs and tubers (potatoes, yams, onions, shallots and garlic)
- spices and condiments
- fish and shellfish
- poultry.

Labelling of irradiated food

Under the Food Labelling Regulations 1996, any irradiated ingredient in food:

- must be marked with either 'irradiated' or 'treated with ionising radiation'.

If such an ingredient is used in food sold in a restaurant, canteen or a place where food is prepared for immediate eating, the same labels must appear on a menu or anywhere else where a customer can see it.

Commercial organisations providing irradiation services to the food

industry must be licensed and have satisfied the Minister that they meet all the relevant safety requirements.

Temperature controls

The Food Safety (Temperature Control) Regulations 1995 contain special rules governing the temperature at which food is to be stored, and apply to all food businesses – manufacturers, processors, distributors, retailers and caterers.

You must ensure that food which may cause health hazards if not properly stored (because micro-organisms or toxins may develop) is kept chilled at temperatures at or below 8°C.

A Guide is available from the Department of Health containing details of the requirements, exemptions and other information about the effect of the regulations.

Food Safety (General Food Hygiene) Regulations 1995

If your business handles food, it is vital that you comply with the regulations about hygiene. Everything you do must be hygienic – including your premises, equipment, transport, people and the produce.

Special care must be taken to ensure that people working with you are properly trained in the basics of food hygiene and personal cleanliness. Work in the food industry covers a wide range and some food handlers need specialised knowledge. The intention is that most people who handle food should have a proper understanding of the following:

● how and why bacteria multiply
● the effects of food poisoning
● how to prevent food poisoning and food contamination
● personal health and hygiene
● how to keep premises and equipment clean
● pest control
● legal responsibilities.

Codes of Practice

The Act enables the Secretary of State to publish statutory Codes of Practice for the guidance of food authorities and traders. Codes (available

from HMSO) have been published covering:

- Inspection Procedures
- Responsibility for Enforcement
- Legal matters
- Inspection, Detention and Seizure of Suspect Food
- Improvement Notices
- Prohibition Procedures
- Sampling for Analysis or Examination
- Food Standards Inspections
- Food Hygiene Inspections
- Enforcement of Temperature Controls
- Enforcement of Food Premises Registration
- Division of Enforcement of Quick Frozen Foodstuffs
- Crown Premises
- Enforcement of Shellfish Regulations
- Enforcement of Fishery Products Regulations
- Food Hazard Warning Systems
- Enforcement of Meat Products Regulations.

In addition, there are very useful guides which anyone running any business involving food should have to hand:

- *Guidance on the Food Safety (General Food Hygiene) Regulations 1995* – available from Health Publication Unit, Heywood Stores, Manchester Road, Heywood, Lancs OL10 0PZ.

- *Caterer's Guide to the Food Safety (General Food Hygiene) Regulations 1995* – from HMSO.

Registration and licensing of premises

If you run any sort of food business, or have a non-food shop but have a cafe, canteen or restaurant, the premises must be registered. The Food Premises (Registration) Regulations 1991 say that it is an offence:

- to use premises for the purpose of a food business on five or more days, whether consecutive or not, in any period of five consecutive weeks – unless they have been registered, either by the proprietor or some other person.

You must apply for registration at least 28 days before the business starts.

Registration also applies to offices and factories which have a kitchen, canteen or dining room.

Exemptions

First, those premises already dealt with by other methods of registration or licensing: slaughterhouses, poultry meat slaughterhouses and cutting premises; meat export cutting premises, cold stores and trans-shipment centres; meat product plants approved for export to an EU country; dairies and dairy farms; milk distribution premises.

Secondly, premises where the activities present a low risk to health: places where game is killed in sport or where fish is taken (but not processed); where crops are harvested, cleaned, stored or packed (but not where the food is packed in the form in which it will finally be sold to the consumer); honey harvesting places; egg production or packing places; livestock farms and markets and shellfish harvesting areas; places where no food is kept (a kitchen only used for washing up, for example).

Thirdly, some vehicles and stalls are exempt: private cars, aircraft and ships; food vehicles based outside the UK; vehicles which are kept at registered premises (or those which are exempt); market stalls provided by the person running the market; tents, marquees, etc.

Fourthly, places where the main activity has nothing to do with food, but where drinks, snacks etc are given to customers without charge; food sold through vending machines; voluntary/charitable organisations where no food is stored (except for tea, coffee, etc.); Crown premises certified exempt on grounds of national security; places providing food or drink during a religious ceremony; national disaster food stores.

Finally, there are very important exemptions for some businesses run from domestic premises – those where the resident is not the owner of the food business, which would cover home-caterers who supply pre-prepared food or meals to someone who then sells them (except where the business involves the peeling of shrimps or prawns is concerned); those where honey is handled and sold; those where crops are produced, cleaned, stored, packed and sold (which would exempt such food sold from a farmhouse – but not if it is sold from a separate farm-shop); and finally domestic premises where bed and breakfast (and/or evening meal) is provided in premises with not more than three bedrooms.

Registration

You have to apply to the appropriate registration authority, which means, in England and Wales, the district or London Borough Council, the Common Council of the City of London or the Port Health Authority (if it is a food authority for the purposes of the Food Safety Act).

You must fill in a prescribed form and give the following details:

- the address of the premises
- the name of the food business
- the type of premises – 17 are specified but any other can be added
- an indication of the type of food handled or food-based activity carried on
- information must be given about the use of vehicles, ships and stalls for preparing, transporting or selling food
- the name of the proprietor – and the manager if different
- the address of the firm's head office or registered office
- the number of people employed.

There is no charge for registration and your application cannot be refused. All changes affecting the premises, the nature of the business or of its management must be notified to the registration authority. It should be borne in mind that the point of the new rules is to ensure that all premises are to be registered; so if a large company has premises in several different local authority districts, registration will be required in each district in which premises are to be found.

The register is open to inspection by the public but the only information to which the public will have free access is the name of the business, the name (if any) and address of the premises and the type of food business. That is all. The authority has a discretion to make a charge for supplying copies of the register. However, there is no public access to the identity of the owner or manager of the premises, which seems an odd way of safeguarding the public!

The food authority may add to the secret part of the register details about offences which may have been committed, the number of and reasons for inspections made to the premises and assessments of the likelihood of risk.

You may find it useful to contact the Department of Food and Rural Affairs, 17 Smith Square, London SW1P 3JH; tel: 0207 238 6000; website: defra.gov.uk; helpline 08459 335577.

Offences

The possible offences are:

- using premises which are not registered
- permitting such use
- failure to notify changes

which carry a maximum fine of level 3 (at present £1,000), and

- knowingly supplying false information

which carries a maximum fine of level 5 (£5,000).

New businesses will usually have to register at least four weeks before the planned opening so that the local authority may arrange for enforcement officers to visit and inspect the premises to give advice on hygiene.

The Food Safety Act 1990 gives wide powers to enforcement authorities in connection with:

- inspection and seizure of suspect food
- the service of a 'detention notice' where it is believed that food does not comply with the safety requirements – or, without an inspection, it appears that any food is likely to cause food poisoning or any disease communicable to humans
- Improvement Notices, which must contain the following:
 - the grounds for believing that the proprietor is not complying with the regulations
 - the ways in which the regulations are being broken
 - the measures which must be taken to enable the proprietor to comply
 - the period (of at least 14 days) in which improvements must be made.The intention is to ensure that unsuitable food premises are brought up to standard but without involving the businesses in unnecessary expense.
- Prohibition Orders may be sought when the local authority is satisfied that there is a risk of injury to health:
 - in the use of the premises for any process or treatment, or
 - the construction of the premises or the use of any equipment, and
 - the state or condition of any premises or equipment used for the business.

"But I thought I could decide which standards were reasonable"

The prohibition may apply to such of the above activities as is appropriate:

- for a court to close down, partially or completely, food businesses which are a danger to the public (exercisable following a conviction for failing to comply with hygiene or food processing regulations)
- for a court to prevent the proprietor of a food business from running any other food business
- to enable emergency action to be taken by an enforcement authority when it believes that there is an 'imminent risk of injury to health'
- for the Government to make an Emergency Control Order if it is satisfied that there is imminent risk of injury to health arising from commercial operations with respect to food, food sources or contact materials of any kind.

Failure to Comply

The following are all criminal offences:

- failure to comply with an Improvement Notice

- failure to comply with a Prohibition Order
- failure to comply with an Emergency Control Order or any directions
- failure to comply with an Emergency Prohibition Notice or Order.

Summary of Key Learning Points

1. The 'general safety requirement' applies to everything that you sell – not merely goods covered by former regulations.

2. You will be convicted if you sell an unsafe product and you failed to co-operate and remove it from sale.

3. Never ignore advice from enforcement officers about dangerous products.

Checklist

☞ Who needs to be aware of safety regulations and how they apply to what we sell? What steps do we take to monitor the safety of goods?

☞ How do we ensure that all relevant safety information is passed on to our customers? Who checks that it is done?

☞ How would we handle a product recall?

☞ Who is responsible for checking the flammability of furnishings and compliance with the regulations?

☞ Do we sell food or have a canteen or restaurant? Are our premises licenced? Who oversees compliance with the food safety laws?

☞ What is our training policy about food? Have all relevant staff been trained?

9

Your Liability For What You Sell

We have looked at the way the law makes you, the retailer, responsible under the Sale of Goods Act 1979. There are other legal duties which apply to you, some of which are covered by the civil law; others come under the criminal law although they have many characteristics of the civil liability.

Negligence

The 'negligence' in this chapter is a legal concept which you must distinguish from its use in everyday language. One of the best definitions was by a judge in 1856:

- 'Negligence is the omission to do something which a reasonable man, guided upon those considerations which ordinarily regulate the conduct of human affairs, would do, or doing something which a prudent and reasonable man would not do.'

Put simply, it is a duty to exercise reasonable care to avoid acts or omissions which can be reasonably foreseen.

This 'duty of care' is owed in two ways. First, for the goods that you sell or the services you supply; secondly, with regard to your premises.

Goods

This duty runs through the chain of distribution. Obviously the person who manufactures goods has the prime responsibility to take reasonable care in their design and in the way the item is made. For things which are inherently dangerous, he must ensure that there are adequate warnings and

instructions about the way they are used and kept, especially where the customer has no reasonable possibility of examining them before he actually uses them.

However, the law says that the duty of care applies to retailers, because you have direct contact with the person who is buying the goods and have a unique opportunity to talk to them about any dangers or risks.

This would cover things which might cause skin problems, such as shampoo, cleaning products or treatments to clothing – or other unwanted results causing damage. Your duty of care is also particularly relevant when children will be the likely users. There have been cases involving letting children use pistols or petrol.

 WARNING: Make sure that adequate information about safe use is passed on to customers.

 WARNING: Take great care when selling children anything which is potentially dangerous. It is better to lose a sale than unwittingly cause a disaster.

As a retailer, you are obviously not responsible for manufacture but you are the person who selects the stock which you want to sell and this means that you should make sure that you use respectable and established

suppliers. Your duty extends not only to customers but also to anyone using goods which they did not buy themselves.

There was a case (*Fisher v. Harrods (1966)*) in which a retailer sold a jewellery cleaning fluid which 'exploded' when used by the purchaser's wife, injuring her eyes.

- The shop was held to have been negligent:
 (a) by failing to make enquiries from the manufacturer
 (b) by failing to have the product analysed
 (c) by marketing it without any warning.

The manufacturer's duty applies to anyone coming into contact with the goods, including carriers and retailers, so you may have redress should you be injured by goods reaching your warehouse.

Services

If you offer to carry out services – for example, dry-cleaning, repairs, servicing cars, building, decorating – you will be assumed to possess the level of skill of an average person doing the particular job.

Under the contract you must do what has been agreed; but your potential liability in negligence means that you must do it properly, making sure that any materials used are suitable, that you employ appropriately trained workers and that everything possible is done to avoid injury or damage.

Premises

You must make sure that any part of your premises to which the public has access is safe. Inside, shops must be well lit and free from obstructions; floors must be level and without hazards such as warn carpets or holes. Above all, you must have a reasonably foolproof and properly administered system of regular inspection to check against spillages and breakages which might cause injury.

Sometimes the law can be confusing. In one case, a supermarket was held not to have been negligent when a customer fell over a pile of cartons four feet high, presumably because she should have looked where she was going (*Doherty v. London Co-operative Society (1966)*).

On the other hand, another supermarket was held liable to a customer

who was injured after slipping on spilled yogurt; the store was unable to show that it had a proper inspection system (*Ward v. Tesco (1976)*). This was followed in a later case where an employee slipped on a patch of tea spilled on the floor of an office – even though the organisation knew about spillages and had put up a notice asking people to take more care (*Bell v. DHSS (1989)*).

These days courts are more likely to find in favour of people who are injured, so, although there may be legal confusion, you do not want to be involved in a test case.

 WARNING: Make sure your premises are safe. Have a laid-down, regular inspection system. Ensure staff know who is responsible for making it work. Check that the system is properly operated.

A lot of problems can be avoided by using commonsense.

One retailer had an escalator in the store. Because children kept fiddling with the 'emergency stop' button, he hid the switch behind a display. A woman fell on the escalator and was injured. Her injuries were worse because no one had been able to find the stop switch. The retailer was liable to her. His reason for hiding the switch was useless.

In another example, someone walked into a glass display unit and was hurt. The reaction of the manager was 'that is the third time this week'. This would be treated as clear evidence of knowledge of the hazard. The retailer would be liable.

Do you have glass counters? If so, do customers rest shopping bags or children on them? Are they strong enough to take such loads? Has a glass top ever cracked or, worse still, broken in the past? If so, you would be negligent, because:

- you owed a duty of care
- you knew of the danger
- you failed to do anything about it.

 WARNING: Any emergency system must be clearly signposted.

 WARNING: If any hazards appear, such as spillages, holes in floors or floor coverings, cracks on counters, lights failing, low beams:
- **tell the public**
- **rope the area off**
- **think about putting a staff member there to warn people**
- **if need be, close.**

Other points to think about

- How often do you have fire drills?
- Do all staff know what they have to do when the fire alarm goes off?
- What do you do if someone phones to say there is a bomb in the shop?
- Are there unlit steps where the public might stray – by accident or design?
- Do you have areas marked 'staff only'?
- If so, could a child (who could not see or read the sign) get in?
- Are public places safe?
- Are your displays stable?
- Could anyone knock them over accidentally?
- Might a child wander into a shelf edge?
- Are glass and china displays within reach of toddlers or babies in prams?

Note: See criminal liability under Health and Safety at Work Act etc. 1974 (below).

Carparks

If you provide parking facilities, they must be reasonably safe and free from hazards such as potholes, broken glass etc which might cause injury to customers (and others) using them.

Contracting out

In the past, many traders have used contract terms or notices to try to limit or avoid liability for their own negligence. These are now controlled by the Unfair Contract Terms Act 1977.

The Act makes void (that is, of no legal effect):

- contract terms and notices in carparks and elsewhere excluding or limiting liability for death or personal injury caused by your

negligence or that of your employees
- any term in a consumer contract limiting your liabilities under the Sale of Goods Act 1979 (see page 50).

The Act says that the 'reasonableness test' (see page 63) will apply (among other things) to:

- contract terms or notices excluding liability for loss or damage (other than death or injury) caused by your negligence.

 WARNING: Any form of words avoiding liability for the consequences of your own negligence is useless if someone is killed or injured.

Breakages by customers

Normally a customer who breaks something in your shop does not have to pay for it. It is just one of those things. However, you can make people responsible by putting up a notice. To avoid arguments it should say words to this effect:

- Please do not pick up or handle goods; ask the staff to help you. If you break anything, you will have to pay for it.

You still have to take care that things such as glass or china are displayed so that an average, reasonable customer would not knock them while looking around the shop.

Criminal sanctions

Most sensible traders will know that they can face prosecution if an employee is injured at work; but they may not realise that they also end up in the dock if a customer is hurt in their shop.

Under section 3(1) of the Health and Safety at Work Act 1974:

- Every employer must conduct his undertaking in such a way as to ensure, so far as is reasonably practicable, that persons not in their employment...are not exposed to risks to their health and safety.

This duty extends to contractors and visitors as well as customers and means that you can be prosecuted if someone is injured in your shop.

For example, in 1995 a store was prosecuted under the Act. A three-

year-old child was bruised and grazed when a built-in oven, which was not properly secured, toppled over as she reached up to the door. When inspectors checked the store some three weeks later, it was found that some ovens were still not secured in their display units.

The company was prosecuted after it was discovered that there had been several similar incidents in which children had been injured. A two-year-old had sustained a fractured skull but, despite this, the company had failed to introduce any new control systems designed to ensure that displays were correctly assembled and that regular checks were maintained.

A cynic might say that if anyone was to blame it was the parents of the child who failed to keep it under control in the store and had either allowed it to fiddle with goods on display or had not bothered to prevent it wandering about. It could be argued that it was an experience from which the child might learn – that even nice, well-lit and interesting places like shops are full of dangers and that it is foolish to play with things you do not understand.

Of course, the company ought to have secured heavy goods like cookers, especially when it was clear that their systems did not work properly.

The outcome for the store was painful; it was fined £15,000 and ordered to pay £700 costs.

 WARNING: Make certain that anything heavy or unstable is properly secured so that it will not topple when handled by an untrained customer.

 WARNING: Look at what happens in your shop; assess the potential risks; install simple control measures before accidents occur.

 WARNING: The maximum fine under the Act is £20,000.

Other aspects of safety

Trolleys

The Environmental Protection Act 1990 contains a sledgehammer to crack a very small nut. Although abandoned trolleys are a problem, they have a

section and a whole schedule to themselves.

By section 99, district councils can put Schedule 4 into force. This has a set of steps to deal with abandoned trolleys – both shopping and luggage trolleys (each exhaustively defined as though magistrates might have difficulty in recognising a trolley when they saw one).

'Wild' trolleys can be seized, removed, retained and either returned to the owner or disposed of; charges may be levied for recovery. If a trolley is on 'occupied' land the council may remove it only with the occupier's consent; otherwise it must serve notice on him.

 WARNING: Deliberately parking a row of supermarket trolleys on a footpath outside a shop can amount to obstruction if they take up an unreasonable amount of space (Devon County Council v Gateway (1990)).

Waste

Everything that you, as a trader, want to dispose of nowadays is controlled by section 75 of the Environmental Protection Act 1990.

There are regulations about:

- 'household, industrial and commercial waste'
- 'household waste' means waste from domestic property, a caravan, a residential home or a school or hospital
- 'Waste' includes '...any substance or article which requires to be disposed of as being broken, worn out, contaminated or otherwise spoiled'.

Your waste will undoubtedly be 'commercial waste' (unless you are a manufacturer, when 'industrial waste' may also be involved). You may need to consider the effect of the Controlled Waste Regulations 1992 which create a new category of waste, not referred to in the Act at all, called 'clinical waste'. This is defined as:

- '... any waste which consists wholly or partly of ... animal tissue ... being waste which unless rendered safe may prove hazardous to any person coming into contact with it ... '

Under these rules you have a 'duty of care' towards the rest of us – and you must do the following:

- store waste safely and securely so it cannot escape
- secure waste which someone else will remove
- make sure it is removed by an authorised person.

In addition:

- You probably need to hand over a written list of the waste.

Product liability

This novel development came to the UK after an EU Directive in 1985. It is made part of our law by Part I of the Consumer Protection Act 1987.

The Act extends the concept of 'strict liability' (as hitherto found in, for example, the law of sale of goods) by making the 'producer' of defective products liable to a person who is killed, injured or suffers loss of or damage to property. 'Producer' includes:

- the manufacturer
- an 'own-brand' retailer, and
- an importer bringing the product into the EU (not necessarily into the UK).

 WARNING: Retailers can be liable as 'producers' where a person affected by a defective product asks within a reasonable time for the name of the manufacturer etc – and the retailer fails to supply details.

'Products' include:

- goods
- component parts
- raw materials
- electricity.

Game and agricultural produce are excluded from the scope of the Act, so long as they have not undergone any process.

How does the Act work?

There must have been a defect which presupposes fault on the part of the producer at some stage in the chain of concept, design, production and distribution.

Despite much comment, claims based on product liability will not be

great; certainly it is unlikely that there will be a flood of actions. Historically, large numbers of victims never pursue claims. They may start an action but drop out without compensation or are bought off at a figure below what a court might have awarded. The Pearson Commission in 1978 (Cmnd 7054) estimated that there might be 30,000 to 40,000 injuries a year caused by defective products other than drugs; at that time the Commission estimated that only 5 per cent of that figure attracted any compensation. Admittedly there has been some change of attitude in the last 10 years or so with the public becoming both more aware of their legal position and being more inclined to make a claim, although it is not clear whether this can be seen in terms of more litigation.

Product liability will allow some people, who previously would have had to prove negligence, to seek compensation for the wrong they have suffered. This would include users of defective products who had no rights against the supplier (who might be the seller or hirer of the goods). However, the victim still has to overcome a substantial evidential burden.

Burden of proof

Although the Act makes no reference to this at all, the victim has to prove:

- the existence of the defect
- the damage suffered, and
- the causal link between the two.

At first glance, this may not seem difficult, but if the case involves electronics or machinery and the accused producer declines to make any admissions, taking the entirely permissible step of requiring a plaintiff to prove his case, the obstacles may be insuperable.

What is a 'defect'?

It is measured by reference to 'safety', which means the risk of danger or damage to people or property.

Contrary to popular belief, a product is not defective simply because it wears out or does not work properly. The test is whether its safety is such as people generally are entitled to expect.

In considering defectiveness, the Act says:

- that all the circumstances shall be taken into account including:
 - the way the product was marketed

- its 'get-up'
- the use of any mark and instructions and/or warnings about how the product is (or is not) to be used
- what reasonably might be expected to be done with it
- that a product is not to be considered unsafe by reason only that a better product was subsequently put into circulation. This rules out using hindsight.

Defences

When the victim has met the initial burden of proof, the defendant has a range of defences open to him. These include that the defect arose because of compliance with any local, national or EU obligation, and that the defendant was not the producer. There is a defence that the supply was not in the course of a business and the defendant was not the producer – or, if he was, that he had no view to profit. This covers the sale of food and other products at village fêtes, etc.

The three most significant defences are these:

- First, that the defect did not exist 'at the relevant time'.
 In essence this means:
 - for manufacturers – when the product left the factory gate
 - for importers into the EU – the time when they supplied the product to someone else, whether wholesaler, retailer or even the end user.

It is for the defendant to establish this but, where a product causes damage, it may be difficult for him to prove that the defect was not present when the product left his factory. Nonetheless, a product may go through many hands and processes after it leaves its place of manufacture and might have become defective because of someone else's act or omission.
 - for electricity – the relevant time is when it was generated, which would rule out claims for damage suffered by consumers when there are power cuts or surges.

- Secondly, there is the 'state of the art' defence.
 This allows a defendant to show that the state of scientific and technical knowledge at the 'relevant time' was not such that a producer of such products might have been expected to discover

the defect (had it existed when the product was under his control).

Again, hindsight is not allowed to benefit the victim. Even though a safer product subsequently appeared, or was in the course of production when the defective one was supplied, the defendant will escape liability. However, it would not be a defence to say that meeting the required level of safety would increase costs.

- The third defence relates to component manufacturers.
 They will be jointly and severally liable with the producer of the finished product unless they can show that although their component failed, it only did so because of some action by the producer of the finished product or because of compliance with instructions given by the producer of the assembled product.

The Act defines 'damage' to include:
- death
- personal injury (including any disease and any other impairment of a person's physical or mental condition)
- any loss of or damage to any property (including land).

Exclusions

The Act excludes:

- economic loss, and also loss of or damage to the defective product itself (apparently because it was thought that the victim would be insured against such losses)
- claims under £275
- contracting out or avoidance of liability between a producer and a victim.

However, the Act does not prevent the adjustment of liability between, for example, a manufacturer of components and the producer of the assembled product.

Other claimants

Although the Act is primarily intended to help individual consumers, there is nothing to prevent other classes of victim – for example, employees, commercial hirers, traders and contractors – to sue in product liability (although their claims for property damage would be very limited).

Summary of Key Learning Points

1. Make sure that adequate information about safe use is passed on to customers.

2. Take great care when selling children anything which is potentially dangerous. It is better to lose a sale than unwittingly cause a disaster.

3. Make sure your premises are safe. Have a laid-down, regular inspection system; ensure staff know who is responsible for making it work; check that the system is properly operated.

4. Any emergency system <u>must</u> be clearly signposted.

5. If any hazards appear (spillages, holes in floors or floor coverings, cracks on counters, lights failing, low beams):

- *<u>tell the Public</u>*
- *rope the area off*
- *think about putting a staff member there to warn people*
- *if need be, <u>close</u>.*

6. Any form of words avoiding liability for the consequences of your own negligence are <u>useless</u> if someone is killed or injured.

7. Make certain that anything heavy or unstable is properly secured so that it will not topple when handled by an untrained customer.

8. Look at what happens in your shop; assess the potential risks; install simple control measures before accidents occur.

9. The maximum fine under the Act is £20,000.

10. Deliberately parking a row of supermarket trolleys on a footpath outside a shop can amount to obstruction if they take up an unreasonable amount of space.

11. Retailers can be liable as 'producers' where a person affected by a defective product asks within a reasonable time for the name of the manufacturer, etc. – and the retailer fails to supply details.

 # Checklist

☞ Are we satisfied that we understand the 'duty of care' which we owe to our customers? Could we prove that we have taken all reasonable steps to check that goods are suitable and safe?

☞ Who is responsible for the safety of our premises? Do we have a clear system for reporting accidents, hazards, spillages, etc.? Who is in charge of it? Do *all* staff know how the system works and who they have to report to? Do they understand the need – and reason – for urgent action?

☞ How often do we have fire drills? When was the last time? Who is responsible? When did we last ask for a fire officer to visit?

☞ Do we have a policy for breakages by customers? How do they know? Are all notices clear?

☞ Who is responsible for monitoring safety at all our premises?

☞ How do we control shopping trolleys, baskets?

☞ What steps do we need to take about waste to comply with the Environment Protection Act?

☞ Have we considered product liability risks in all our buying decsions?

10

The 'Due Diligence' Defence – What It Means

The only way in which the legal concept of 'due diligence' as a defence, and the way prudent traders can make use of it, is to have a look at the decisions made by the higher court when cases have gone on appeal. This chapter contains a review of a range of reported cases. When you read them, remember the principles apply across the board – not just to businesses under the various headings.

The 'absolute' offence

Normally in a criminal trial the prosecution has to prove that the person accused of an offence was guilty beyond reasonable doubt. If a defendant pleads not guilty, the prosecution has to prove that the material facts in the case are true. It is also necessary to show that the defendant intended to break the law (what is known as 'mens rea').

However, despite this general rule there are a number of offences created by Acts of Parliament which contain an absolute prohibition against doing something. These are known as 'absolute' offences. In these cases it does not matter that the person accused did not intend to break the law. The mere fact that there is clear evidence that the Act in question has been contravened is sufficient for a conviction to be inevitable.

This 'absolute' or 'strict' liability can cause injustice if a person was held to have committed an offence for which he had no responsibility at all, or because of an accident or some cause completely beyond his control. So to be fair, a defence is normally included in consumer protection statutes containing absolute offences. This has come to be known as the 'due diligence' defence.

Examples are contained in:

- s.24 Trade Descriptions Act 1968
- Consumer Protection Act 1961 (now repealed)
- Consumer Safety Act 1978 (now repealed),
- s.168 Consumer Credit Act 1974
- s.34 Weights and Measures Act 1985
- s.39 Consumer Protection Act 1987

Trading Standards and other enforcement authorities are familiar with the principles by which such a defence may be permissible. Each of these Acts contain a 'by-pass' provision so as to enable the real culprit to be brought before the court even though a retailer was found in possession of the offending goods.

The gist of the 'due diligence' defence is that someone else was responsible, but you, the person accused, did all you could to avoid the offence.

Virtually all the forms of words are standard but, as an example, this is the text of the defence in section 24(1) of the Trade Descriptions Act 1968:

- … it shall … be a defence for the person charged to prove -
 - (a) that the commission of the offence was due to a mistake or to reliance on information supplied to him or to the act or default of another person, an accident or some other cause beyond his control, and
 - (b) that he took all reasonable precautions and exercised all due diligence to avoid the commission of such an offence by himself or any person under his control'.

 WARNING: For the statutory defence to be successful, you must have taken positive action; you cannot simply sit back and do nothing and expect to be able to convince a court that you acted reasonably.

Looking at the law reports, it is clear that:

- 'reasonable precautions' involves setting up a system to ensure that things will not go wrong
- 'due diligence' means seeing that the system works properly.

Although you may say that the offence arose through someone else's act,

omission or mistake the onus is on you to prove that both points have been established.

'Due diligence' and the courts

Where you claim that the offence was due to the act or default of, or to reliance on information supplied by, another person you must serve written notice on the prosecutor identifying that person at least seven days before the hearing.

Lawyers and judges always say that each case depends on its own facts. This is true, but the courts always look at previous similar cases in which the higher courts have considered whether the defence was used successfully by the defendants.

The leading case is *Tesco Supermarkets Ltd v. Nattrass (1972)* where the main issue was the ability of a company accused under the Trade Descriptions Act 1968 to rely on the 'act or omission of another person' – in that case a shop manager. He had failed to supervise a young employee arranging packets of washing powder which were marked with a higher price than that for which they were for sale. The House of Lords acquitted Tesco. The decision has been criticised because it allows a company to avoid criminal liability for an offence committed by its own local manager. It is said that, where an offence shows a failure of control within a company, it is better for the company to be prosecuted.

One judge said that what amounts to the taking of reasonable precautions and the exercise of due diligence depended on all the circumstances of the business carried on. In another case (*Garrett v. Boots Chemists Ltd (1980)*) it was said that what might be reasonable for a large retailer might not be reasonable for the village shop.

Cases about retailers

Sherratt v. Geralds the American Jewellers (1970). The shop sold a 'waterproof' watch which filled with water after an hour in water. Its reliance on the reputation and experience of the wholesaler was rejected by the court which said that the shop had taken no precautions. Just dipping one watch in a bowl of water would have revealed the problem and would have avoided the offence.

Sutton LBC v. Perry Sanger & Co. Ltd (1971). Dog-dealers sold a dog as a 'Sheltie' which was in fact a cross-breed. They were not experts in Shelties, and said they had relied on the description given them by their supplier, coupled with an unsigned pedigree certificate and the fact that a vet had not denied that the dog was a Sheltie. The Appeal Court rejected this view and said that because they were dealers, what they had to do to prove 'due diligence' was all the greater. No precautions had been taken and no diligence exercised.

Haringey LBC v. Piro Shoes (1976). A shop sold shoes marked 'all leather' which were not entirely made of leather. Head office told the branch manager in writing that he must ensure that no shoes were sold with the wrong label. A pair of shoes was sold and the word 'all' crossed out at the till. The Appeal Court said that the company ought to have told the manager to ensure that the false label was removed before the shoes were put on display because that was when the offence was committed.

Urwin v. Toole (1976). Under the Weights and Measures Act 1963 an employee of a coal merchant was stopped. His lorry was carrying a sack of coke not bearing a quantity label as required by the Act. Although sacks were normally checked each morning they had not been on the day in question;

employees were instructed to report missing labels. The Appeal Court held that the coal merchant had not shown that the label was missing because of an accident, nor that there was a proper system of regular checking.

Garrett v. Boots Chemists Ltd (1980). Boots were accused of an offence under the Pencils and Graphic Instruments (Safety) Regulations 1974. They said that they had notified their suppliers about the regulations and had made it a condition of their order that pencils should meet the standards in the regulations. The Court said that what might be reasonable for a large retailer might not be so for a village shop. A company as large as Boots should have taken a random sample, whether statistically controlled or not. Not doing this was a failure to take reasonable precautions.

Turton v. United Co-operative Ltd (1992). Retailers were accused of two offences under the Furniture and Furnishing (Fire) (Safety) Regulations 1988; displaying chairs which did not carry the appropriate display labels, and three dining chairs whose seat pad covers failed to pass the 'match test'. The chairs had permanent labels saying that the covers were not match-resistant. The seat covers of the dining chairs failed the match test.

Knowing that new regulations were coming into force, the retailers tried to get rid of all stock which did not meet the new rules and told staff to refuse any item not carrying a batch number and a swing ticket showing compliance with the regulations. However, the manager had not read the permanent labels; had he done so he would have removed the chairs from the shop.

The Appeal Court held that the labels clearly indicated that the chairs broke the law. Reading the notice was an elementary precaution which would have been reasonable. Failure to do so showed that the defence had not been made out.

Robert Gale v. Dixons Stores Group Ltd (1993). A computer which had previously been sold by retail, but had been returned, was sold again as 'new'. The store claimed to come within the defence because their manager had failed to comply with in-house instructions. However, the Appeal Court was told that there was no proper system in operation to check returned goods to see whether they were faulty at the time of the offence. One was set up eight months later which, if followed, would have avoided the offence.

Cases involving wholesalers and importers

Taylor v. Lawrence Fraser (Bristol) Ltd (1977). The accused had supplied toys painted with a substance containing excess lead in breach of the Toys (Safety) Regulations 1974. Although their defence was that the manufacturers had given them a written undertaking that the goods met regulations (and that local Trading Standards Officers had been asked to take samples at any time for analysis), the Appeal Court held that there was no effective guarantee. The traders had done nothing except try to pass their responsibility onto the enforcement authorities.

Riley v. Webb (1987). This case involved the supply of 'secretary sets' which also broke the Pencil and Graphic Instruments (Safety) Regulations 1974. The trader told the court that order forms contained a condition that orders were placed on the understanding that the goods met any relevant statutory requirements. Having dealt with the supplier for many years, having a small staff and a large number of lines, the trader argued that to make random samples would have been unreasonable. The Appeal Court held that they could have taken a simple step to avoid their present trouble by asking for a specific assurance about the goods in question; or they could have imposed contract terms by which their suppliers would have had to ensure that the Regulations had been complied with. By merely imposing a general term, they had failed to take precautions.

Balding v. Lew Ways Ltd (1995). A wholesaler supplied a toy which infringed the Toys (Safety) Regulations 1989. It had an accessible protrusion which was not so designed to reduce the risk of injury. The defendants' sales director knew of the regulations but it was found that:

- there was no test against the British Standard
- there was no test to see if the toy met the safety regulations
- there was no evidence that the defendants had asked its independent analysts whether the British Standard in the certificate issued with the toy complied with the regulations;
- the certificate was not produced to the bench
- the defendant had warranted to retailers that the toy complied in all respects with the law.

It was held that there was not due diligence without further enquiries from

the analysts; whether an analyst was competent would depend on the instructions he received. The defence could not be made out if analysts had not been asked if the toy complied with the law of the land.

Hicks v. Sullam Ltd (1983). The importers supplied light bulbs to British Home Stores. A defective bulb was falsely described. They had imported 110,000 from the Far East but none which were supplied to British Home Stores had been tested. There were no sampling procedures for safety tests and no independent test reports were obtained which might have revealed the serious fault. The only steps which the defendants took was to employ two firms in Taiwan and Hong Kong to check bulbs, a procedure which had been satisfactory in the past. Since the defect had arisen, the defendants had set up a sampling system.

On appeal the defence was rejected. The absence of both a random sampling system and independent expert examination in the UK showed that no precautions were being taken. Reliance on foreign checking was insufficient.

Rotherham MBC v. Rayson (UK) Ltd (1988). Importers of Far East goods supplied a packet of crayons bearing a false trade description ('poisonless') which contravened the Pencils and Graphic Instruments (Safety) Regulations 1974. The importers gave suppliers details of statutory requirements and asked that only adverse reports should be sent to them. None had been received. From an annual supply between 7,000 and 10,000 dozen packets of 12 crayons only one packet was chosen for analysis. The sample had complied.

The Appeal Court held that the method of reporting back only adverse analysis through agents did not prove that such tests were taking place. Sampling in the UK of one packet out of 10,000 dozen did not meet the required standard. Trying to make a manufacturer responsible did not show compliance with the defence.

P & M Supplies (Essex) Ltd v. Devon County Council (1992). An importer was accused of breaking the the Toy (Safety) Regulations 1974 with a soft toy which came in a variety of versions with different numbers of legs. The company had a turnover of £8 million of which £4.5 million was attributable to toy sales. It had some form of in-house testing by certain staff and samples were taken at random. Over £13,000 was paid for a public analyst to test soft toys.

Out of a total of 76,960 toys imported from China only 378 (0.49 per cent) were randomly tested. The company claimed that this met the defence. For the prosecution it was said that it was for a trader to establish, first by independent statistical evidence or otherwise, that his testing system was adequate to deal with the type and number of goods involved; and then show that the testing system in practice was carried out scrupulously.

Although the Appeal Court upheld the conviction it added that magistrates should be helped with independent statistical evidence to show how a reasonable trader could avoid committing an offence.

Other cases

Kinchin v. Haines (1979). A coal merchant was prosecuted for selling coal underweight (there was a deficiency of nearly 1.25 cwt in 1.5 tons of coal). His lorry had been loaded with sacks which were out in the rain. The trader knew that as the moisture evaporated, the weight would decrease. Although it was argued that he could only offset the loss by overweighing, the Divisional Court held that he should have tried to obtain the correct weight and that to do nothing could never amount to 'taking precautions'.

Barker v. Hargreaves (1980). A dealer sold a car described as in 'good condition throughout' which had corroded floor panels hidden by undersealing and by the battery. He had obtained an MOT and relied on the standard wording on the MOT certificate: 'A test certificate should not be accepted as evidence of the satisfactory mechanical condition of a used vehicle offered for sale.'

His conviction was upheld. There was no system for checking the condition of used cars and by merely referring to the disclaimer on the MOT certificate he had neither taken any precautions at all nor exercised any diligence.

Need for systems and training

Baxters (Butchers) v. Manley (1985). Butchers were accused of offences involving short weight and false pricing. These were due to the act or default of their shop manager and the company relied on the statutory defence. In rejecting the claim the court held:

- the company did not establish that it had taken positive precautions to avoid an offence – their meat checking and record

system was only introduced after the offence in question
- no regular checks were made by the district manager and supervision was inadequate
- although new rules were sent to shops, no instructions or guidelines were given to managers – this indicated lack of due diligence
- the shop manager only made two visits to the company's residential training school; this was insufficient for his position within the company; refresher courses were seldom used.

Knowsley MBC v. Cowan (1992). A retail butcher had ten shops; at one he employed an experienced manager. A 15-year-old boy was taken on by the manager as an assistant and given some training in the use of scales, slicers and tills. The boy made a series of errors relating to the weight and price and labelling of meat. The butcher said that he gave his managers instructions about the selection and training of staff but the court held that they were given no guidance. There was no system for checking the age of applicants and no formal training; neither was there any supervision of recruitment or training. The butcher had not met the defence.

Successful Use of Statutory Defence

It is possible to meet the defence. In *Westminster City Council v. Turner Gow (1984)* coal merchants were charged with short weight offences which were the fault of their driver who was convicted. For its part, the company relied on the statutory defence and was acquitted.

On appeal the court held that the company had displayed sufficient diligence:

- they had prepared written instructions for all drivers
- a copy was displayed in the weighbridge office, another given to each driver
- the driver in question admitted that he had deliberately disobeyed clear orders which he knew
- there was a system of checking at the weighbridge and this infringement only occurred two months after the notice was first displayed.

A lot of cases involve winding back the mileage on a car's odometer.

Lewin v. Rothersthorpe Road Garage Ltd (1984). A car salesman admitted applying a false trade description relating to the odometer; his

employer pleaded the statutory defence successfully and satisfied the magistrates on three points:

- they had adopted the Motor Agents' Association Code of Practice drawn up in consultation with the Office of Fair Trading
- they had instructed their salesmen in the operation of the Code of Practice
- that instruction was reinforced by regular meetings of salesmen where the importance of observing the Code was emphasised.

Machine failure

How do you fare when normally reliable machinery does not do its job properly? This is of great importance for all involved in any industry where many processes are undertaken by machine but where great accuracy is required for the chemical content of materials and for final weight. In *Bibby-Cheshire v. Golden Wonder (1972),* a manufacturer was prosecuted for selling short weight crisps. It was able to satisfy the statutory defence by showing:

- that the bags of crisps were filled by machines; that they used the best available machines but that none was sufficiently accurate to produce no underweight bags;
- that it was economically impossible to weigh individually 20 million bags a week;
- that there was an efficient system of random checking which ensured that no machine consistently produced underweight bags.

Exceptional circumstances

Hurley v. Martinez & Co. Ltd (1990). A retail wine merchant obtained a quantity of German wine from an importer. Although the vineyard had its own state-approved laboratory for the analysis of alcohol content, the wine in question was tested at another state-approved laboratory where it was found to contain 7.17 per cent alcohol. By an error of an employee at the vineyard when ordering labels, the wine was labelled showing an alcoholic content of 8 per cent rather than 7 per cent or 7.5 per cent.

Neither the importer nor the retailer made any test of alcoholic content; the retailer did not ask the importer or the vineyard for details of the state-approved laboratory analysis carried out in Germany.

The prosecution had suggested that one bottle ought to be sampled from each batch of wine; the magistrates had thought that this was not reasonable for a small retailer dealing with reputable suppliers. Then it was said that the retailer ought to have called for the test certificates and compared them with the labels; the court was not convinced that this would have eliminated the risk of mislabelling of the sort in this case. The Appeal Court held that the wine was subject to a tight regime enforceable under EU law of which independent verification formed an integral part.

Carrick District Council v. Taunton Vale Meat Traders Ltd (1994). A meat inspector wrongly stamped a carcass as fit for human consumption. The council argued that the due diligence defence could only be made out if a defendant had devised a fool-proof and independent system to avoid acts or defaults by employees and that the trader could not rely on any action of the meat inspector. The Appeal Court rejected that submission and held that where it was reasonable for a trader to rely on the inspector's certificate there had been 'due diligence'.

Hereford and Worcester County Council v. T & S Stores Ltd (1994). Enforcement officers told a 12-year-old girl to buy cigarettes from the defendants' shop. The magistrates found:

- that the assistant was not supervised at the time of the sale
- that instructions had been given about the legal requirements by written bulletins advising what staff should do if they believed a customer was under age
- the sales person knew of the law and the written instructions
- that each shop had a procedures manual updated each week which required managers to ensure staff read it
- area managers checked on a regular basis.

The court held that the defendants' procedure was sufficient to ensure that all reasonable steps were taken to avoid an offence.

Berkshire County Council v. Olympic Holidays Ltd (1994). At a travel agency, a consumer was shown the price of a villa holiday on a VDU screen which carried the words 'Warning: this is not a confirmed reservation'. A second screen was then called up which showed the final price. There was no warning that the price was not to be relied on. The screen carried a display 'confirm booking' and 'confirm costing'; from

this screen a printout was made. The words quoted denoted confirmation of booking and costing, not that they remained to be confirmed.

The brochure price was £182 more than what was shown on the screen and an invoice for that higher price was sent to the consumer. The company's terms and conditions contained the words:

> 'In the event of a costing error being given either by our reservations/ viewdata system or appearing on the confirmation/invoice, the price/ costing as it appears in the brochure or late availability circular will prevail. The company undertakes to refund to the client any overcharge caused by such an error.'

The court held that the brochure price would prevail over the screen and:

- that Olympic Holidays undertook substantial testing of the software before it was used and the court did not think its accuracy could be further checked
- that the software was correct and when the transaction was repeated the correct information was given
- such a fault had not happened before
- although 'nonsense' was sometimes displayed, it had never been known for the screen to show information that was incorrect
- that an unexplained fault, unconnected with the software, caused the incorrect display
- the fault might have been caused by a fault on the telephone line connecting the mainframe to the agency
- no one would ever know the cause for certain.

The court found that the use of the disclaimer on the screen, the tests and the fact of no previous fault meant that the company had taken all reasonable steps and exercised all due diligence to avoid committing the offence. However, costs were refused to the company because the bench thought that they had brought the case on themselves by refusing to honour the screen price and refund the £182 but had offered the consumer the choice of cancellation.

The court also found that it was standard practice in the travel business for agents to rely on screen prices as being the final price and not refer to brochures for final prices. Booking forms were signed on the basis of screen prices. Any disclaimer on the second screen would confuse.

Summary of Key Learning Points

1. For the statutory defence of due diligence to be successful, you must have taken positive action; you cannot simply sit back and do nothing and expect to be able to convince a court that you acted reasonably.

 Checklist

☞ Do we provide adequate supervisions to limit possible risks and errors?

☞ What precautions do we take to avoid legal difficulties?

☞ Do we have established systems of regular checking of products, labelling, premises, posters, advertisements, etc.?

☞ Are our management systems and controls complete? Do we have 'standing instructions'? Whose responsibility is it to check that systems are used and understood by all staff?

☞ Do we have comprehensive training for all staff covering legal duties and responsiblities?

☞ How regularly are all staff given refresher courses?

11

How To Use Hazard Prediction And Quality Control

You should be reassured by noting first that the reported decisions represent only a tiny proportion of the total prosecutions brought each year; and secondly that in almost every judgment the courts are at pains to emphasise that each case depends on its own facts.

The objective of enforcement authorities is to identify and prosecute those who are really responsible for offences. Food items which fail to meet statutory requirements are discovered either when a member of the public complains or when enforcement officers make test purchases – either at random or following complaints. Most potential offences are discovered at the retail end of the chain of distribution. The enforcement authority has to decide whether the retailer is culpable or whether to use the 'by-pass' provisions.

Whether or not you are prosecuted may well depend on the way your business methods stand up to scrutiny. Knowledge of the importance of good practice is much more likely to convince an enforcement officer that you are doing all you can to avoid breaking the law. What conclusions can be drawn by analysing the cases discussed in the last chapter?

Now we shall look at the steps you need to take in order to be able to show – should the need arise – that you have indeed:

- taken all reasonable precautions, and
- exercised all due diligence.

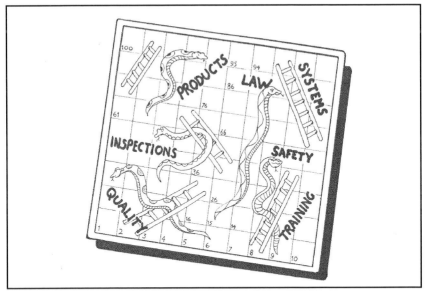

Due diligence

Any intention to make full use of the concept of 'due diligence' means a complete re-think of the way in which any given business is run. A manufacturer must be able to show not only that his products come off the assembly line at a reasonable price but that he cares about his choice of materials, methods of manufacture and packaging to ensure that they meet the highest standards of safety. All concerned have an interest in seeing that the best possible systems of production control are devised, put into operation and are thereafter continuously monitored.

The size of the system will obviously be geared to the type of business. You must take great care to see that the purpose of any system is clearly defined. While it is easy to devise one which turns out any required product, it is useless if the product itself is unsatisfactory. Good systems ensure both that production lines work efficiently and the end products themselves meet statutory requirements.

There are three basic requirements for systems:

- they must be able to predict and analyse the hazards commonly associated with the business
- there must be controls to eliminate these hazards

- the controls themselves must be monitored properly.

For example, are there well-established and respected Codes of Practice in general use your trade sector? You should be able to show that you are both aware of and follow them.

In addition, it is essential that companies operate written instructions for the setting up, monitoring and control of systems; and for there to be paper-based records of supervision, training, sampling, audits and checks. This applies to everyone involved throughout the chain of distribution.

The first you may know of a problem is when an enforcement officer calls. Retaining these written records and orders, invoices and delivery notes for a reasonable period enables you to have available tangible evidence of the system on which you rely to establish due diligence.

Retailers

The larger the company, the greater its responsibilities. However, all retailers have much to do and they must put into operation two-pronged systems. The first of these applies vertically through the company:

- they must be able to show from the Board down that senior managers are aware of current safety, hygiene, labelling and quality regulations and published Codes of Practice
- they must prepare information and guidance for all key staff at buying, distribution and branch functions
- they must operate a careful system for the selection of managers and see that control is exercised to make sure that proper steps are taken to ensure compliance with the law
- adequate supervision must be provided at all levels, from board, to area, district and branch
- training is a fundamental requirement and refresher courses essential.

The second limb relates to their sources of supply:

- they must show that they use reputable suppliers
- they must undertake random sampling of all types of goods supplied and make regular visits to the suppliers to carry out hazard and safety 'audits'
- they might demand that their suppliers provide them regularly with the results of their own in-house sampling tests

- that they require suppliers to provide evidence that they follow accepted Codes of Practice and use effective quality and quantity control procedures
- that they require suppliers to maintain systems of 'positive reporting' – that is, that regular reports are sent by the suppliers confirming that all manufacturing processes are working properly (rather than only reporting when problems arise)
- that they require suppliers to provide written confirmation that their products meet the quality required.

Own-brand labelling

Many large retailers stock items which bear their own labels although they are manufactured, packed and labelled elsewhere by another company. These retailers may have considerable influence in the design of products, choice of raw materials, flammability, chemical and electrical properties, what standards are to be followed and how the product is to be packaged and labelled.

Those who sell own-brand products must appreciate that the more they impose their own demands upon the factory, the more likely they are to be taken as being responsible for the product in its final form on the shelf. They will not be able to avoid prosecution by blaming the manufacturer or importer.

Wholesalers

Wholesalers have been prone to prosecution for other consumer protection offences because they have tended to be responsible for the selection of stock and the range of goods which are available to small retailers. They may be able to rely on the statutory defence and point to the act or default of their suppliers.

Importers

It may not be appreciated that importers are as much affected by the law as everyone else, although their function may appear to be limited to making administrative arrangements for goods to be brought from abroad into the UK. As the person responsible for the goods until they reach the manufacturer or retailer, an importer must ensure that he is aware of all relevant safety, composition and quality legislation in this country.

Small-scale retailing

Small retailers are only likely to be prosecuted if they have themselves failed to meet the principal consumer protection laws – e.g. dirty premises, selling tainted food, short weight, misleading labelling or false trade descriptions. This would seem to be the right approach by enforcement bodies.

Sampling – warnings

In *Hicks v. Sullam,* British Home Stores avoided prosecution by showing that they used a reputable supplier – although that firm was convicted for lack of sample testing. One could argue that BHS was in no different a situation than Boots in the *Garrett v. Boots* judgment where Boots was guilty for failing to undertake sample testing. The obvious conclusion:

- it is safer to undertake random testing – thus showing positive precautions being taken – than risk being criticised for doing nothing.

In a number of cases, defendants had tried to show that they had relied on sample testing by other people either in the UK or abroad. This was not attractive to the courts. Foreign companies operating abroad are beyond the risk of prosecution and so cannot be punished for putting British consumers at risk.

- For imported goods, it is always better for the UK company to institute its own testing.

Finally, using contract terms to impose the duty of compliance with regulations on the supplier does not amount to the taking of all reasonable precautions.

Food Distributors

Distributors must ensure that vehicles, drivers and all food handlers comply with hygiene regulations. Refrigerated vehicles must meet both domestic and European temperature controls. Again, systems must exist to ensure supervision, training and control at all levels.

Food offences

In the case of prepacked food, or other food which is unsafe before it reaches the small retailer (the loaf with a piece of metal in it), the offence is not the responsibility of that retailer, though his shop may be cited as the place of offence. So long as he uses reputable suppliers whom he can identify by keeping proper records, proceedings would almost certainly be taken against the supplier or manufacturer as the actual offender.

 WARNING: Even the smallest food retailer must be able to show that he is aware of current legislative requirements for food safety, hygiene, composition and quality and that he takes adequate steps to inform and train his staff – and to carry out in-service refresher courses.

If, nonetheless, the retailer is prosecuted, then so long as he neither manufactured nor imported the offending food, there are special defences in sections 21(3) and 21(4) of the Food Safety Act 1990 which say that he is 'deemed' to have exercised due diligence.

 WARNING: If you change the state of the food supplied to you, you may not be able to rely on the special defences for retailers

Conclusions

Looking at the cases in Chapter 10, it is plain that in most of them the defendant had either failed to do anything, or had tried to shift the burden on to someone else. Judgments show, over and over again, that only positive action will satisfy a court that a person knows and understands what is meant by taking all reasonable precautions and exercising all due diligence.

It will mean the continuous assessment of risks and the allocation of resources to eliminate them. Having demonstrably sound systems will have two distinct advantages.

- First, higher standards of safety mean that the risk of unsafe goods being supplied to the public by accident or neglect is kept to the minimum. This will prove to the consumer that the company is concerned only to sell what is the best.
- Secondly, the risk of prosecution is reduced to a minimum.

The larger the company the more important it is to demonstrate workable systems of control and of the selection and training of staff. Moreover, a constant awareness of the need to take all possible steps to avoid breaking the law is required.

For everyone engaged in production, manufacture and distribution it cannot be overemphasised that concentration on quality and safety is a paramount consideration and one which will be scrutinised by the courts whenever the statutory defence of 'due diligence' is set up.

The courts recognise that human beings are fallible and that the best designed and operated systems may fail. They do not expect perfection; they do expect a determination on the part of those involved in manufacturing and retail distribution to take all steps possible both to ensure that what they do is safe and that it complies with all legal requirements.

12 Golden Rules

1. Find out about the current law relating to the safety and description of everything you sell.
2. Keep up to date on changes and improvements in the law.
3. Establish contact with the Chief Trading Standards Officer for your area and explain to him that the company wishes to keep ahead of its legal obligations.
4. Random testing – for safety, materials, size and weight, labelling.
5. Never assume that any product or printed material conforms to statutory requirements.
6. Consider establishing quality control systems – using BS5750 or ISO 9000 or similar certification.
7. Establish hazard prediction controls – follow HACCP (Hazard Analysis of Critical Control Points).
8. Ensure that all systems are continuously monitored.
9. Ensure the continuous assessment of risks and the allocation of resources to eliminate them.
10. Be prepared to justify testing procedures, hazard prediction systems and monitoring.
11. Do not believe that contract terms requiring suppliers to comply with legal duties will protect.
12. Ensure that all safety, assembly and use instructions are in a language which consumers can understand.

Enforcement

Most consumer protection laws with criminal sanctions – for example:

- Trade Descriptions Act 1968
- Consumer Credit Act 1974
- Weights and Measures Act 1985
- Consumer Protection Act 1987

are policed by Trading Standards Departments of county councils, London borough councils and regional councils in Scotland.

For those connected with food and hygiene enforcement, it is divided. The Environmental Health Departments of district councils investigate:

- food contamination by micro-organisms
- some chemical contamination where there is an immediate risk to health
- contamination by mould and foreign bodies.

Trading Standards at county councils deal with:

- chemical contamination, improper use of additives
- compositional offences, adulteration and misleading claims.

The Health and Safety at Work Act etc. 1974 is administered by members of the Institute of Shops, Health and Safety Administration.

In addition to any special powers which they may have (for example, in relation to food), all enforcement officers are given powers to enable them to investigate complaints properly. They are allowed to:

- make test purchases
- search premises
- examine the way goods are produced
- demand the production of records
- seize and detain goods
- make copies of records.

When checking Sunday opening, they are allowed to:

- measure premises and take photographs.

When will you be prosecuted?

Contrary to popular belief, Trading Standards Officers and Health Inspectors are primarily concerned with helping traders get things right. They do not want to spend their valuable time hanging around courts unless it is absolutely necessary. Therefore whether or not you are prosecuted will depend on many factors – for example:

- the seriousness of the offence
- your previous record
- the likelihood of the 'due diligence' defence being successful
- whether there are cooperative witnesses
- your willingness to prevent any repetition
- how much the public would benefit from a court case
- whether there is other suitable action
- what your explanation is for the offence.

Checklist

☞ **Quality control systems:**

- They must be able to predict and analyse the hazards commonly associated with the business.
- There must be controls to eliminate these hazards.
- The controls themselves must be monitored properly.

☞ **Retailers need to follow these rules. First:**

- They must be able to show from the Board down that senior managers are aware of current safety, hygiene, labelling and quality regulations and published Codes of Practice.
- They must prepare information and guidance for all key staff at buying, distribution and branch functions.
- They must operate a careful system for the selection of managers and see that control is exercised to make sure that proper steps are taken to ensure compliance with the law.
- Adequate supervision must be provided at all levels, from board, to area, district and branch.
- Training is a fundamental requirement and refresher courses are essential.

☞ **Secondly, sources of supply:**

- They must show that they use reputable suppliers.
- They must undertake random sampling of all types of goods supplied and make regular visits to the suppliers to carry out hazard and safety 'audits'.
- They might demand that their suppliers provide them regularly with the results of their own sampling tests.
- That they require suppliers to provide evidence that they follow accepted Codes of Practice and use effective quality and quantity control procedures.

 # Checklist

- They require suppliers to maintain systems of 'positive reporting' – that is, that regular reports are sent by the suppliers confirming that all manufacturing processes are working properly (rather than only reporting when problems arise).
- They require suppliers to provide written confirmation that their products meet the quality required.

☞ **Follow the 12 Golden Rules**

1. Find out about the current law relating to the safety and description of everything you sell.

2 . Keep up to date on changes and improvements in the law.

3. Establish contact with the Chief Trading Standards Officer for your area and explain to him that the company wishes to keep ahead of its legal obligations.

4. Random testing – for safety, materials, size and weight, labelling.

5. Never assume that any product or printed material conforms to statutory requirements.

6. Consider establishing quality control systems using BS5750, ISO 9000 or similar certification.

7. Establish hazard prediction controls: follow HACCP (Hazard Analysis of Critical Control Points).

8. Ensure that all systems are continuously monitored.

9. Ensure the continuous assessment of risks and the allocation of resources to eliminate them.

10. Be prepared to justify testing procedures, hazard prediction systems and monitoring.

11. Do not believe that contract terms requiring suppliers to comply with legal duties will protect.

12. Ensure that all safety, assembly and use instructions are in a language which consumers can understand.

12

When Things Go Wrong

You will have to be able to deal with three situations when things go wrong:

1. something goes wrong which is either your fault or your responsibility
2. your suppliers let you down
3. customers cause problems.

1. Your fault or responsibility

You will know by now that you have legal obligations to sell goods which are reasonably safe, which are of a satisfactory quality and fit for their intended use. Your premises must be safe. If you provide services, you must do them to a reasonable standard, in time and at a fair price.

Nonetheless, you will inevitably sell something which is brought back with claims that it is defective. What do you do?

The first thirty seconds of a complaint are often the most important, because in that time the attitude of the trader and customer will become apparent. If you are tired, harassed, overworked and anxious and (in human terms quite understandably) snap at the customer you may trigger a series of events which will only be ended in the court room.

Complaints systems

Every trader, large or small, must have a well-thought-out complaints procedure with which all staff are familiar. You should ensure that customers with complaints are seen by someone whose attitude is, at worst, neutral.

Most people who complain are unhappy about the situation. They may

be angry or upset or embarrassed. They will probably expect the worst and come to you prepared for an argument. The first thing you can do is to defuse those feelings:

- smile at them and when they tell you that the goods are broken or do not work, say you are sorry
- take them somewhere private and help them relax
- ask them to explain what the trouble is
- ask to see the item so that you can form a preliminary view of the problem.

" Defuse those feelings"

Do you sell that sort of article? If so:

- do not say that the customer could not have bought it from you
- do not begin by demanding proof of purchase. Assume – at first – that the customer would not be complaining to you unless he bought the item from you
- ask when the customer bought the goods and whether he can remember the sales assistant
- if the defect is obvious and the purchase was in the previous few weeks, ask the customer what he wants.

 WARNING: Many customers do not want their money back. They want a replacement. Your legal duty is to give a refund. If you offer a replacement, make sure that you record in writing that this is what the person asked for and was happy with. That avoids problems.

If the goods were bought some time ago, it may be that the customer has 'accepted' them under section 35 of the Sale of Goods Act 1979 (see page 87). In this case, his right to reject the goods and claim a refund has been lost for ever.

 WARNING: You may still be liable to compensate a customer – for the cost of a repair, travel, loss of pay, etc., or a lump of money – to make up for the fact that the item was not as good as it should have been.

A dented fridge, for example, still works perfectly well as a fridge but is not very nice to look at. A settee with a missing button can still be sat on but may not be repairable. A £20 note can work wonders.

Where does the manufacturer fit in?

The legal responsibility for the goods is yours alone. It is not your fault that they are defective but the Sale of Goods Act 1979 makes you liable to the customer through the contract you made. If this means that you have to make a refund and take back the goods, you have a similar remedy against your supplier (subject to the terms and conditions in the contract – see page 50).

From a customer's point of view one of the most infuriating things a retailer can say is that the problem must be referred to the manufacturer before any decision can be made. Regulation 16 of the Sale and Supply of Goods to Consumers Regulations 2002 has changed the law. Manufacturers' guarantees will have contractual effect to the extent of the terms offered.

 WARNING: Do not engage in buck-passing. Accept your legal responsibility.

Remember, too, that if there is a genuine dispute about what went wrong, the goods themselves are the best evidence that the customer has. If he parts with them, he loses control of the most crucial part of any legal case

he has to bring. He cannot know what may be done to the goods while they are in the manufacturer's hands; even during transit they may be further damaged.

 WARNING: It is usually unreasonable to expect a customer to part with goods so that you can send them back to the manufacturer.

Guarantees have some benefits (see page 36) but they are not a substitute for the rights given to your customers by the law.

 WARNING: Do not fall into the trap of telling the customer to use the manufacturer's guarantee.

Proof of purchase

There are crooks who go round stealing things from shops and then go back to ask for refunds. Despite what you read, they are few and far between. If you have any doubts, you can ask a person making a complaint to let you have some sort of proof of purchase.

 WARNING: If this is the way you deal with complaints, you must provide customers with something tangible as a receipt, invoice or sales docket which they can recognise for what it is.

 WARNING: Any receipt, etc., should carry your name and address and the date of purchase should be clearly legible.

If there is no receipt, etc., the customer may have a cheque stub, credit card voucher or a guarantee card which would link the goods with you.

Proof of defect

As I have said, you are liable if you realise that there is something inherently wrong with what you have sold. The fault may not be obvious or you may suspect that it was caused not by some inherent defect but by some action by the user. The customer may have done something unwittingly.

A washing machine may overflow because a filter is blocked with fluff, not because there is anything wrong with the machine. Curtains may have faded because unsuitable fabric has been used in a very sunny window. A

radio may not work because it was dropped or left out in the rain.

- In such cases, you are perfectly within your legal rights to refuse to do anything until the goods have been examined more carefully to establish the reason for the fault.

There is a long-standing legal rule that puts the burden of proof in a lawsuit on the person making the claim. The important questions which the customer has to be able to prove are:

- what is wrong?
- what caused it?

If you do not accept liability, tell the customer so in a civil way explaining that he can take the matter to court.

 WARNING: Do not be afraid to reject a complaint – so long as you believe you are not liable.

Codes of Practice

Section 8 of the Enterprise Act 2002 enables the OFT to approve codes of practice to look after the interests of consumers. For many years, there were many approved codes covering a wide range of trade sectors.

All has now changed. All existing approved codes have been brought to an end. The OFT wants trade associations to re-assess their existing codes and to re-draft, where necessary, to ensure that they meet core criteria laid down by the OFT. There are several important new aspects to the whole process. Associations will have to show that they have consulted consumer and enforcement and advisory services when drawing up the code and, even more significantly, in the more formal approach to monitoring the code in operation. Codes must deal with truth in advertising, clear information both before a contract and in any terms and conditions in an agreement. Delivery dates and cancellation rights must be covered, as well as any guarantee, pre-payment protection and after-sales service.

Above all, the complaints-handling machinery – covering both redress and compliance systems – must be transparent and independent with a majority of lay people involved in any appeals procedure.

Trade associations will have to ensure that there is the widest publicity

of the code, and that it is available free. When a code is approved by the OFT, the association will be able to use an OFT logo.

Details of the core criteria and the progress of applications for approval can be found on the Office of Fair Trading website: oft.gov.uk

The OFT's address is, Fleetbank House, 2-6 Salisbury Square, London EC4Y 8JX.

Complaints procedures summarised

- Every shop should have a staff member trained to deal with complaints.
- Make sure staff do not deny that they could have sold items.
- All staff should be told over and over to refer complaints to the complaints person.
- The complaints person should have discretion to make refunds up to a limit of, say, £200.
- An unjustified complaint should be rejected politely with a straight-forward explanation.
- Make staff realise that a complaint is not a reflection on them; they should never take complaints personally.
- The complaints person must have full information about the relevant Code of Practice and any Conciliation service.
- Try not to overrule a decision by the complaints person.
- Above all, deal with complaints quickly.

 WARNING: Remember that one dissatisfied customer can do a great deal of damage by telling his friends and relations what a rotten deal you gave him.

Giving money back

When confronted by an irate customer, offering him money can work wonders. It deflates his anger. He may be complaining because he wants to make a point rather than become involved in a legal process.

Under the Sale of Goods Act 1979, a customer who rejects goods with good reason is entitled to his money back, plus any out-of-pocket expenses such as travel or loss of pay. You should make sure that he gets his money as quickly as you took it from him when he bought the offending goods.

If he has lost the right to reject because he has had the goods for a 'reasonable time' and has therefore 'accepted' them (see page 82), the

customer may still be entitled to compensation ('damages') if goods become defective.

 WARNING: If someone complains months after purchase that there is something wrong, do not dismiss it. The right to claim money remains open.

Section 53 of the Sale of Goods Act 1979 says in summary:

- where there is a breach of (contract) and the buyer is not ... entitled to reject the goods he may:
 - (a) (claim a) diminution or extinction of the purchase price – this means that if the goods are repairable or the damage is cosmetic, he can claim some money but not the price he paid, or if they are damaged beyond repair he can claim the whole price; or
 - (b) (sue) for damages – these are calculated as the estimated loss directly and naturally arising, in the ordinary course of events, from the breach of (contract), including what is popularly known as 'consequential loss'.

2. Your suppliers let you down

There are two main ways in which you may have a grievance against your supplier:

- when you have put in an order and he fails to deliver the right goods by the agreed delivery date
- when you have to accept responsibility to your customer for defective goods but the supplier refuses to meet your claim.

Just as your customer has rights against you, the Sale of Goods Act 1979 applies equally to you – with one major difference. The contract which you make with your supplier may contain small print by which he excludes or limits his liability to you (see page 57). This is one of the reasons why it is so important to understand how to negotiate the contract at the outset to try to ensure that you protect yourself.

Most arguments between traders and suppliers are resolved without involving lawyers, but if all else fails it may be inevitable that you use the Unfair Contract Terms Act 1977 to challenge 'exclusion' clauses. Remember, the Act says that:

- terms avoiding liability for loss, etc., arising from the supplier's negligence or breach of contract
- terms avoiding liability for breach of contract (including/excluding consequential loss), and
- terms allowing him not to perform the contract at all

are only legally acceptable if they are 'fair and reasonable' (see page 59).

3. Customers cause problems

Customers may fail to pay for what they buy or to take delivery. You can sue them – see below.

Customers may break things. As we have seen (see page 164), there are ways in which you can make it clear that they have to pay for breakages.

Customers may behave badly in the shop. You are perfectly within your rights to ask them to leave; if they refuse you may use such force as is appropriate to require them to leave.

You may believe that a customer is stealing. If you have reasonable grounds for this belief, it is best to call the police immediately. Doing this may enable you to avoid any claim for compensation if the person is acquitted by the court or is proved not to have stolen anything.

 WARNING: If you use a 'citizen's arrest' and prevent the person leaving the shop, you run a serious risk if your belief proves to be groundless.

 WARNING: If you do stop a suspect – get the police straightaway.

Anyone who is stopped from leaving your shop or is physically restrained without good reason may bring a claim against you for damages for 'false imprisonment' or 'trespass' and, if they are put in fear, 'assault and battery'.

Getting it wrong can be expensive. For example, a 15-year-old was followed from a shop, stopped in public and wrongly accused of shoplifting. His bag was searched and he was forced to go back to the shop. He was held for 15 minutes, then the police took him home where evidence was produced which cleared him. (Damages agreed at £1,000 (*Ward v. H Turner (1992)*).

A nurse was detained by a store manager on suspicion of passing a forged banknote. She claimed she was forcibly restrained and suffered injuries which affected her career. Although the shop denied liability it agreed to pay damages of £60,000 plus costs (*Robinson v. Dorothy Perkins (1992)*).

A lady was challenged by a store detective and accused, her bag was searched but nothing was found. She left the store but later returned to make a complaint. While with the manager, the detective returned with an item he claimed she had stolen. The police came, she was arrested and held in cells for 3½ hours, then released and not charged. Damages assessed at £2,000 for wrongful arrest and false imprisonment plus £500 aggravated damages (*Spark v. Appraisal Security Services (1994)*).

- Get to know your local Crime Prevention Officer and take advice on how to protect your shop and stock.

Other problems you may encounter

Restrictive Practices
You have to watch out that your trade association does not impose on its members any agreement containing restrictions on prices, the method of doing business, or carves up the area in which business is to be done and the pool of customers available to members. Such agreements – which must be registered with the Office of Fair Trading – may fall foul of the Restrictive Practices Act 1976. The test is whether the restrictions are in the public interest.

Retailers may make informal arrangements which are also illegal. Local traders may agree to divide territory or to charge the same price for services. This is just as much a restrictive agreement as those decided at national level. They should be registered, or better still avoided like the plague.

Anti-competitive practices
Analogous to restrictive agreements are attempts made to influence you or to prevent you being competitive. Manufacturers may try to lay down the price at which you sell their goods to the public. Other terms may also be found – for example:

- only supplying goods to chosen retailers

- banning you from selling goods from a rival manufacturer
- making you carry the full range of products
- requiring the sale of one product to be tied to another product
- imposed recommended prices
- withholding supplies
- loyalty bonuses and rebates.

If you are threatened with any sanction or refusal of supply, you should contact the Office of Fair Trading which can take action against the supplier under the Competition Act 1998.

Small claims in the county court

A wise man once said: 'Arbitrate, don't litigate.' Litigation is to be avoided at all costs. The only winners tend to be the lawyers.

If all else fails you may end up in court – either suing your customer because he did not pay you, or facing a claim for damages for defective goods or service.

Where a case is brought in the county court for a claim not exceeding £5,000 and is defended, it will almost always be treated as an 'arbitration'. The case goes through all the usual steps up to the hearing before the District Judge, but this may be held less formally. The strict rules of evidence may be ignored and the judge may want to see the site. Where the dispute is about defective goods or services, the judge will want to see a report from an independent expert. Without this, the person bringing the case will be unable to proceed.

Experts are thin on the ground, and are expensive. Customers may have to choose between bringing a case and paying perhaps more than the amount at issue for an expert's report and giving up. Traders can call on their trade association for the names of suitably qualified experts. Some associations will offer technical support for members.

There are rules about costs in 'small claims' designed to discourage the use of lawyers. The loser will not be ordered to pay the winner's solicitor's fees – just the court fee, expert's fees and witness fees.

The time taken for litigation and the risks involved can make Code of Practice arbitration much more attractive.

Suing your customers

It is inevitable that you will have bad debts. Some customers' cheques will 'bounce'. Others will not pay. Retailers often complain that having ordered goods specially, a customer will refuse to take delivery and claim that he does not have to pay. This is not so. If the customer fails to meet the obligations which the law places upon him, you are quite within your rights to sue for the money.

 WARNING: It is an offence under s.40 Administration of Justice Act 1970 to harass a debtor.

The Act says that you must not threaten or alarm someone who owes you money, or make false claims that criminal action may be taken or issue bogus 'legal' documents demanding money.

Crisis Management

In any business activity there always lurks the danger of an catastrophe. It is difficult to prepare for anything which by its very nature is unexpected. However, one sign of an efficient business operation is to have plans to cope with a sudden disaster. These days with food scares, Legionnaires' Disease, glass in babyfood and unsafe products you may be the next victim.

It is essential to have a simple plan of action which everyone knows how to put into operation. This means that all staff know who to contact and, above all, how; it is useless if you keep your home phone number secret. The designated people need to know, as well, the names and contact points for fire, health and medical services. With some disasters minutes can be vital and there should be no delay in telephoning the relevant emergency departments.

The public relations fallout for a company which gives the impression of being in a muddle, slow to respond or uncaring can be long-lasting – *even if the problem is not of its making.*

The press thrives on catastrophes. Your system must be designed to ensure that *you* do not first learn of the problem when a reporter phones you or thrusts a microphone under your nose. This means that you must be able to tell the press what has happened, what you are doing about it and

the immediate consequences both to the public and your employees. Nothing is worse than managers who refuse to talk to the press, say 'no comment' or look shifty or panicky.

This is what you need

1. Make sure all staff have all your phone numbers and are encouraged to contact you day or night in an emergency.
2. Ensure that the police/fire/local council know who has a key.
3. Have immediately to hand phone numbers of enforcement, fire, health and safety authorities.
4. Find out the extent of the emergency.
5. Notify your suppliers.
6. Know the number of the nearest Poisons Unit.
7. Be ready to tell the press, television and radio all about the problem; do not wait to be 'doorstepped'.
8. Trace all affected products.
9. Warn all people likely to be affected.
10. Advise and reassure people not affected.
11. Say how sorry you are and that everything is being done to put things right.

Summary of Key Learning Points

1. Many customers do not want their money back. They want a replacement. Your legal duty is to give a refund. If you offer a replacement make sure that you record in writing that this is what the person asked for and was happy with. That avoids problems.

2. You may still be liable to compensate the customer – for the cost of a repair, travel, loss of pay, etc., or a lump of money to make up for the fact that the item was not as good as it should have been.

3. Do not engage in buck-passing. Accept your legal responsibility.

4. It is usually unreasonable to expect a customer to part with goods so that you can send them back to the manufacturer.

5. Do not fall into the trap of telling the customer to use the manufacturer's guarantee.

6. If this is the way you deal with complaints, you must provide customers with something tangible as a receipt, invoice or sales docket which they can recognise for what it is.

7. Any receipt, etc., should carry your name and address and the date of purchase should be clearly legible.

8. Do not be afraid to reject a complaint – so long as you believe you are not liable.

9. Remember that one dissatisfied customer can do a great deal of damage by telling friends and relations what a rotten deal you gave.

10. If someone complains months after purchase that there is something wrong, do not dismiss it. The right to claim money remains open.

11. If you use a 'citizen's arrest' and prevent a person leaving the shop, you run a serious risk if your belief proves to be groundless.

12. If you do stop a suspect get the police straightaway.

13. It is an offence under s.40 of the Administration of Justice Act 1970 to harass a debtor.

 # Checklist

☞ **Complaints systems – and how to deal with irate customers:**

- The first thing you can do is to defuse those feelings.

 Smile at customers and when they tell you that the goods are broken or do not work, say you are sorry.

 Take them somewhere private and help them relax.

- Ask them to explain what the trouble is.

- Ask to see the item so that you can form a preliminary view of the problem.

- Do you sell that sort of article? If so:

 Do not say that the customer could not have bought it from you

 Do not begin by demanding proof of purchase; assume – at first – that the customer would not be complaining to you unless he bought the item from you.

- Ask when the customer bought the goods and whether he can remember the sales assistant.

- If the defect is obvious and the purchase was in the previous few weeks, ask the customer what he wants.

☞ **Complaints procedures summarised**

- Every shop should have a staff member trained to deal with complaints.

- Make sure staff do not deny that they could have sold items.

- All staff should be told over and over to refer complaints to the complaints person.

- The complaints person should have discretion to make refunds up to a limit of, say, £200.

- An unjustified complaint should be rejected politely with a straight-forward explanation.

- Make staff realise that a complaint is not a reflection on them; they should never take complaints personally.

Checklist

- The complaints person must have full information about the relevant Code of Practice and any Conciliation service.

- Try not to overrule a decision by the complaints person.

- Above all, deal with complaints quickly.

☞ **Crisis Management**

- Make sure all staff have all your phone numbers and are encouraged to contact you day or night in an emergency.

- Have immediately to hand phone numbers of enforcement, fire, health and safety authorities;

- Find out the extent of the emergency.

- Notify your suppliers.

- Know the number of the nearest Poisons Unit.

- Be ready to tell the press, television and radio all about the problem; do not wait to be 'doorstepped';

- Trace all affected products.

- Warn all people likely to be affected.

- Advise and reassure people *not* affected.

- Say how sorry you are and that everything is being done to put things right.

Appendix 1 - List of Addresses

Association of Manufacturers of Domestic
Electrical Appliances (AMDEA)
Rapier House
40-46 Lambs Conduit Street
London WC1N 3NW

Association of British Travel Agents (ABTA)
55?57 Newman Street
London W1P 4AP

Vehicle Builders and Repairers Association
102 Finkle Lane
Gildersome
Leeds LS27 7TW

Society of Master Shoe Repairers
21 Station Road
Desborough
Northants NN14 2SA

Retail Motor Industry Federation
201 Great Portland Street
London W1N 6AB

Scottish Motor Trade Association
3 Palmerston PLace
Edinburgh EH12 5AQ

Textile Services Association
7 Churchill Court
58 Station Road
North Harrow
Middx HA2 7SA

Radio, Electrical and Television Retailers' Assn (RETRA)
1 Ampthill Street
Bedford MK42 9EY

Qualitas Furnishing Standards
Maxwell Road
Stevenage SG1 2EW

Mail Order Traders' Association
Drury House
19 Water Street
Liverpool L2 0RP

National Association of Funeral Directors
618 Warwick Road
Solihull B91 1AA

British Photographic Association
Ambassador House
Brigstock Road
Croydon CR7

Direct Selling Association
29 Floral Street
London WC2E 9DB

Glass and Glazing Federation
44?48 Borough High Street
London SE1 1XB

British Holiday & Home Parks Association
6 Pullman Court
Great Western Road
Gloucester GL1 3ND

Direct Marketing Association
1 Oxenden Street
London SW1Y 4EE

Society of Motor Manufacturers and Traders
Forbes House
Halkin Street
London SW1X 7DS

London and Provincial Antique Dealers Assn
535 Kings Road
London SW10 0SZ

British Shops and Stores Association
2 Main Road
Middleton Cheney
Banbury
Oxon OX17 2TN

Apparel and Textile Confederation
5 Portland Place
London W1B 1PW

Federation of Bakers
6 Catherine Street
London WC2B 5JW

Dairy Trade Federation
19 Cornwall Terrace
London NW1 4QP

Food and Drink Federation
6 Catherine Street
London WC2B 5JJ
British Office Systems and Stationery Federation
6 Wimpole Street
London W1M 8AS

British Retail Consortium
69?79 Fulham High Street
London SW6 3JW

British Standards Institution
389 Chiswick High Road
London W4 4AL

Coal Merchants' Federation of Great Britain
Victoria House
Southampton Row
London WC1B 4DH

Trading Standards Institute
351 London Road
Hadleigh Essex SS7 2BT

Food and Drink Federation
6 Catherine Street
London WC2B 5JJ

British Office Systems and Stationery Federation
6 Wimpole Street
London W1M 8AS

British Retail Consortium
69-79 Fulham High Street
London SW6 3JW

National Federation of Retail Newsagents
Yeoman House
Sekforde Street
London EC1R 0HD

British Standards Institution
2 Park Street
London W1A 2BS

Domestic Coal Consumers' Council
2 Bunhill Road
London EC1Y 8LL

Coal Merchants' Federation of Great Britain
Victoria House
Southampton Row
London WC1B 4DH

Institute of Trading Standards Administration
351 London Road
Hadleigh Essex SS7 2BT

Institute of Shops, Health & Safety Acts Administration
23 Grand Avenue
London N10

Appendix 2 - bssa books

RETAIL SELLING

How to Achieve Maximum Sales

by Peter Fleming

(192 pages, £12.99)

This is a practical guide for all retail salespeople. It shows you how to improve your sales and increase customer satisfaction.

With more than 100 performance tips, 14 case histories, 16 mini-assignments and 11 self-test questionnnaires, this book is really a complete training course in just 192 pages. Every retail salesperson should have a copy.

Peter Fleming, founder of his own consultancy business, won a major travelling scholarship at the age of 19 on the strength of his sales skills in fashion and household textiles. Graduating into the training profession, he managed the training function in Selfridges and has trained countless sales people and managers through public courses, in-company assignments and training publications.

Here, he shares the successful methods he has learned from frontline experience and case histories of clients, including such companies as BMW, Courts Furnishers, Contessa, Moss Chemists, Dunhill, Equator, Moss Bros., Allders International and Alpha Retail.

'This book gives the sales person a great opportunity to develop key skills which will help them achieve success in this crucial job. I have no hesitation in recommending it to you.'

Tim Daniels, Managing Director, Selfridges

To order this book phone Management Books 2000 on 01285-771441 – credit card orders accepted on Visa or Mastercard, or visit their website - www.mb2000.com.

MANAGING RETAIL SALES

How to lead and motivate the sales team and manage the retail business

by Peter Fleming

(220 pages, £12.99)

MANAGING RETAIL SALES is the third book in this series of guides for the retail sector, published in association with the British Shops and Stores Association. In this book Peter Fleming concentrates on the management of retail sales. Packed with case studies, self-assessment exercises and performance tips, this book will provide an invaluable resource for all retail managers, whatever their age or experience. Areas covered include:

- Making the transition from shopfloor to retail manager
- Team leadership/management skills
- Creating the right sales environment
- Customer care – handling customer complaints
- Stock control
- Security, health and safety
- Recruitment and staff development.

Here, Peter shows successful approaches he has used and witnessed from frontline experience and research with companies such as John Lewis Partnership, Flannels Group, The Body Shop, Argos, Williams and Griffin, Beatties, Furniture Land, Marks and Spencer and IBM.

'Managing a retail business becomes more demanding year by year. I welcome Peter Fleming's book for newly appointed and experienced managers.'

Peter Still, Managing Director, John Lewis

To order this book, phone Management Books 2000 on 01285-771441 – credit card orders accepted on Visa or Mastercard, or visit their website - www.mb2000.com.

RETAIL BUYING TECHNIQUES
How to source and plan a winning product range

by Fiona Elliott and Janet Rider

(224 pages, £12.99)

For any retailer, the acquisition of the right stock at the right price at the right time is crucial to the economic well-being of the business. RETAIL BUYING TECHNIQUES, the fourth title in this series of management guides for the retail sector published in association with the British Shops and Stores Association, covers every aspect of the all-important buying function. It is packed with case histories and performance tips and will be exceptionally valuable to everyone in the industry with some responsibility for buying. Subjects covered include:

- Planning the budget
- Planning the structure of the merchandise range
- Developing the product and brands
- Sourcing and buying the product
- Presenting and promoting products profitably
- Improving buying performance.

Fiona Elliott and Janet Rider, are both established retail consultants with extensive experience in buying and merchandising. Between them they have worked for a wide range of companies including well-known retail chains and both are frequent visiting presenters at **bssa** specialist buying courses.

'Good buyers who can build the perfect product range for their market are always in demand. This book will make an important contribution to the better understanding of any buyer's work making it essential reading for all executives.'
John Hoerner, Chief Executive, The Arcadia Group

To order this book, phone Management Books 2000 on 01285-771441 – credit card orders accepted on Visa or Mastercard, or visit their website - www.mb2000.com.

THE RETAILER AND THE COMMUNITY
Inspirational techniques for marketing the business and enhancing its profile

by Peter Fleming with Karen McColl
(242 s, £12.99)

Are you looking for ways of raising the profile of your business in the community? This book provides tried and tested ways of marketing and growing the business with over 90 tips, 10 checklists and 40 case histories.

Written with the busy Executive or Proprietor in mind, the book seeks to explode some of the myths attached to business development and focuses on practical ways of expanding business at relatively low cost. Subjects covered include:

- Making your business stand out
- Researching your market
- Socially responsible retailing, taking an ethical stance
- Getting involved in your community
- Your community working for you
- Advertising – an investment in sales.

"This book shows us how the retailer is an integral part of the wider community. We exist to serve our communities and will profit from the relationship … and this text will make a major contribution to this effort"

Sir John Banham, Chairman, Whitbread Group plc

Peter Fleming, retail consultant, and Karen McColl, researcher, have broken new ground with this detailed and highly inspirational book. Sir John commends this book to you and the whole retail community. Don't miss out! Every retail manager should read it before others gain the competitive advantage. Add it to your bookshelf now!

To order this book, phone Management Books 2000 on 01285-771441 – credit card orders accepted on Visa or Mastercard, or visit their website - www.mb2000.com.

Appendix 3

Training Schools & Short Courses

The **bssa** provides an annual training programme with the sole aim of developing the competence and skills of retail staff and proprietors. Many of these programmes complement the contents of this book – the following are particularly relevant.

Retail Managers and the Community - the workshop from the book

How to gain business benefits from 'community activities' and raise the profile of the business. All firms can benefit from this self-marketing approach!

Course provider: **PFA International for bssa**

Retail Law for Managers – the seminar from the book

A one day seminar designed to increase a manager's understanding of the requirements of retail law. This informative programme offers a full briefing on essential statutes and regulations.

Key Topics

Legal essentials for a contract
Advertising and display of goods
Do's and don'ts of price marking
Trade descriptions – how to avoid 'over-selling'
Complaints policies – how to handle disputes

Course provider: **PFA International for bssa**

Introduction to Buying – practical training course based on the book: *Retail Buying Techniques*

Delegating responsibility to untrained personnel can feel like giving someone else a blank, but signed, cheque! Buying can be a high-risk activity as the stakes are high.

However, formal training limits the risks of over-stocking and poor merchandise selection, and heightens the chances of increased profits. Buying requires skills – not just flair and creativity!

Key Topics

Assess strengths and weaknesses of trade and identify sectors of the market

Gather and utilise sales and stock control data on which to plan buying decisions – when and how to order basic stocks

Plan and manage an 'open-to-buy' budget

Build a merchandise range plan and 'model' stocks

Analyse legal and commercial relationships between suppliers, retailers and customers

Negotiate a case with a partner.

Course provider: **PFA International for bssa**

All the above events can also be provided on an In-Company basis – as well as 'open' training events.

Oxford Summer School – a 7-day Residential School

Tuition and syndicate exercises are provided on topics from buying to business finance and store layout

Key Topics:

Analysis of profit and loss accounts

Generation of cash flow

Decision-making on stock, sales and orders

Effective management styles

The new sore opening plan

A 5-year profit profile

Marketing an organisation

Keynote speakers and tutors from the Retail Industry lead this event for bssa

Index